"You must be the change
you wish to see in the world."

~ Gandhi

Also by Gregory Sass

If I Tell You, Will I Feel Less Scared?

"A moving document. This little book should be read by every teacher and parent in the land." ~ Roy MacSkimming, *The Toronto Star*

"Emotionally powerful." ~ Marg Csapo, *The Vancouver Sun*

"Thank you, Gregory Sass, for leading the way."
~ Marilyn Powell, *The Globe & Mail*

Redcoat

"A compelling story." –James Gellert, *Canadian Literature*

"*Redcoat* is a gutsy little book... a compulsively readable story."
~ Tim Wynne-Jones, *The Globe & Mail*

Growing Toward the Light

"Poignant and cathartic." –*Verse Afire* (Canadian Poetry Magazine)

Shadows

"*Shadows* is a gift to poetry lovers who demand new and inspiring insights." –*Verse Afire* (Canadian Poetry Magazine)

Soul's Journey

by

Gregory Sass

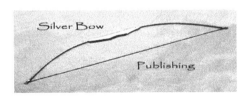

720 Sixth Street, Box # 5
New Westminster, BC
CANADA V3L 3C5

Title: Soul's Journey
Author: Gregory Sass

Cover photo by Gregory Sass: "Woodend," the southernmost point of the Bruce Trail and Niagara Escarpment in Ontario

Cover Layout and design: Annabelle Bann
ISBN 9781774033258 (Print)
ISBN 9781774033265 (Ebook
© 2024 Silver Bow Publishing

Library and Archives Canada Cataloguing in Publication

Title: Soul's journey / by Gregory Sass.
Names: Sass, Gregory, author.
Identifiers: Canadiana (print) 20240470699 | Canadiana (ebook) 20240472098 | ISBN 9781774033258
   (softcover) | ISBN 9781774033265 (Kindle)
Subjects: LCGFT: Autobiographical poetry.
Classification: LCC PS8587.A3847 S68 2024 | DDC C811/.54—dc23

To Annabelle Bann and all young people today:
As you and the Earth experience profound change,
keep the faith, live an examined life,
risk being yourself, and become wise.

Also, to Christopher Hassell and Mary Jane Little
with gratitude for our friendship.

And a big "thank you" to Allan Briesmaster for your
wise counsel and encouragement.

CONTENTS

Preface / 9

1 Dangerous times / 11

2 In the dark wood /49
- Coming back / 57
- Sacred passage / 69
- Living with sorrow / 85
- Stepping into larger shoes / 99

3 Before it is too late / 111
- Solitude / 125
- Four seasons / 135
- The natural history of capitalism / 143

4 God is a metaphor / 163
- God is a metaphor / 163
- Six sermons / 181
- How do I envision / 193

Preface

The Second World War and its aftermath shattered my family and the context in which we lived. Since then, I have been searching the graveyard of my memories for the fragments that are me and tried to reassemble them into a soul—no longer a stranger to myself.

This psycho-spiritual journey through a troubled world has become my home. I have learned that the goals of my life are: to find meaning in it; to try to know that which is larger than me; to give to the world what is uniquely mine to give; and, at the end of my life, to value what this journey was about.

The suffering of the world has also made me a poet and led to a powerful engagement with our predicament. Poets are people who could take the easier path but do not. They resist and are sometimes dangerous because to them life is sacred. They embrace anguish yet insist *this must change.*

Soul's Journey is a collection of new and earlier poems arranged to tell the story of my inner life lived at a significant turning point in human history. Writing this account has been an act of profound remembering and healing. ~ ***Gregory Sass***

1

Dangerous times

The ideal subject of totalitarian rule is not the
convinced Nazi or the convinced Communist
but people for whom the distinction between
fact and fiction...and the distinction
between true and false...no longer exist.
—Hannah Arendt

Dangerous times

Finally, there was no one to confide in.
Distant cries for help
hung noiselessly in the air.
Who was calling and why?
Were they echoes of fear?
Good reasons to be afraid?
You were alone with terror and distrust.
Soon, this was the way it was—
your new life. Everyone looked away
and said things were getting better.
People became indifferent.
There was no resistance.
Some swallowed their principles
and joined the party. A few did not.
Their silence was circumspect.
Men in leather coats knocked
on doors and pushed their way in—
asked questions to which
there were no acceptable answers.
Arrests, concentration camps, and
administrative deaths were now common.

Why?

They were fearful
but thought themselves exalted.
They felt betrayed
and hated in return.
They were conditioned to obey
and became servile as well as tyrannical.
Then war, subjugation, and extermination
seemed logical.
Today we learn
that these characteristics have a
significant (around fifty per cent)
genetic influence.

1938

dark clouds cross her
face
she is here
and then not here
I reach up
grasping
nothing
life is a string of losses
I am your grief
and you become mine
I am the ground
onto which
your tears fall

During the war

he cheated on you often,
demanded a divorce,
cleaned out the bank accounts,
on his last leave made you pregnant again,
and then disappeared at the Russian front.

Meanwhile, in Berlin,
the Americans bombed us during the day,
the British at night.
And you gave birth to my brother—
a weak, sick baby.

In that paralyzing moment
when a bomb explodes nearby,
you held us tightly. You always
whispered, "Not us! We want to live."

My father,

kindly though he seems
in the two photos
I have of him,
was remote and knew me only
through the viewfinder of his camera.
I wish he had held me more.

In war,

the expectation of death
makes men want to beget children.
Yet they leave, and we are alone.
And our world remains unsafe.

My parents' burden

My mother's mother died
when she was four,
and, similarly, my father's father
died when he was four.
Each was wounded by this loss,
and I know that my mother
spent the rest of her life
looking for another mother—
sometimes in the wrong places.
Oddly, I lost my father
when I was four.

1943

Imagine a place
where if you say
the war is lost,
you're beheaded —
or if you're Jewish, "asocial,"
homosexual, Roma, Sinti,
communist, Jehovah's Witness,
you disappear.

The woman next door
tells my unpredictable mother,
who is actually a believer,
"Keep your head down
and your mouth shut
and you'll be alright."

What instruction do you
give your child
about what to say,
how to behave,
what questions not to ask
—to be a bystander?

The photo

"Millions of dead"
is incomprehensible,
but the effect of a single face—
freckled and evincing a simple, touching charm—
is not.
If she had survived,
who would she be now?

Profile of a killer

He was an ordinary man,
a human being.
Working-class.
Often, too old for military service.
An iffy Nazi.
During executions, he was covered
with blood and brains.
He drank to stifle his horror.
He became mute,
and what had happened in the forest,
taboo.
Nothing could stop his nightmares.
Evil gnaws the inner man.

After the shooting,

the surface of the sand-covered mass grave
continued to move
as those not yet dead
tried to claw their way out.
"You get used to killing,"
one policeman thought to himself.
Still, even willing killers were sometimes relieved
when the deportations were orderly,
the executions went smoothly,
and no one resisted.

Thoughts of an eighteen-year-old-soldier

The snow is stained red with blood
but your face is colourless.
Lying there dead and motionless,
you could be me.
Out there in no man's land,
a wounded Russian moans.
They didn't tell us this could happen—

That we might lie there shot,
with nobody to help us.
Neither side takes prisoners
and kills the others' wounded.
It's them or us.
If you're shot and left behind,
you'll have to solve that problem for yourself.
And always hide your anxiety
so that the others don't think you're a coward.
I stare up into the night sky
and think about home.
I haven't prayed since I was a child,
but I do now.
Every day I remain alive
is a good day,
and I'm grateful for it.

1944

December

"Be practical,"
they make light
in Berlin,
"and give a coffin
for Christmas."

The sinking of the *Gustloff*

She was built for six hundred passengers.
This day—January 30, 1945—10 000 refugees
and wounded soldiers were crammed
into every nook and cranny of the ship.
Half were children.
They had spent weeks in freezing weather
escaping the advancing Russian armies.
They were exhausted and grateful to be saved.

At noon, the *Gustloff* cast off.
The dock still thronged with those left behind.
Everywhere there were abandoned baby buggies,
carts, wagons, sleds filled with once-precious belongings.
On the ground lay snow-covered, bundled,
dead bodies stacked like cordwood.
There were some angry shouts and tears of despair.

On board, when the cabins were full,
people bedded down everywhere—
in the music hall, the movie theatre,
the lounges, the dining rooms, the empty swimming pool,
and, finally, on the stairs and in the hallways.
Young mothers paced carrying frozen dead infants
in their arms soothing them,
believing they were still alive.
The loudspeakers tried to connect

lost children with their mothers.
The kitchen produced gigantic amounts of pea soup.

Outside, the air temperature was minus 20 Celsius.
A snowstorm started to rage,
and the deck of the ship iced over.
The small torpedo boats escorting the ship
were overwhelmed by huge waves and were sent back.

On the bridge, the atmosphere became quiet and tense.
There were disagreements about speed, the route,
whether to use running lights, and the location of Russian U-boats.
Below deck, it started to stink terribly.
Many were sea-sick; everyone was gasping for air.
People were exhaustcd and preparing to bed down.

At 21:15 a deafening explosion shook the ship.
Then a second. The lights went out.
And then a third, louder one.
Huge masses of water poured in. The ship listed,
and people, unbolted furniture, and open suitcases slid with it.
Everywhere people stampeded to the upper decks
and trampled those who fell.
On the outer deck, people slipped helplessly and fell overboard.
Others jumped and froze to death.
Bodies wearing life jackets floated everywhere.

As the bow disappeared under water
and the stern reared mightily into the air,
people in the half-filled lifeboats and floats flailed to get away.
In that moment, all lights came on.
The ship's sirens sounded and then became quieter
as the funnel disappeared beneath the waves.
The muffled screams of those on board rose to one last wail of terror.
The time was 22:15.

Everywhere floated dead bodies.
Those of children had their heads under water
and their feet sticking out of it.
A young woman swam up to a full lifeboat.

She lifted her child out of the water and pleaded,
"Please take my child." No one moved.

In the darkness a little boy cried,
"Where is my Mami, where is my Mami?"
Someone in another boat shouted that she'll come soon.
Then only the wind howled.
As God dies, so do we. *

This was the worst maritime disaster in human history. Fewer than one thousand people survived.

The trek out of Dresden

It was bitter cold.
There was a meter of snow,
and the icy wind howled.
She dragged herself from tree to tree
along the road
and stepped over bundles of frozen children.

She wanted to sit down and rest
but the stiff bodies with their glassy eyes
warned her off.
Gabi whimpered.
She tried to nurse her.
The baby didn't latch.
The milk in the bottle was like ice
and she wouldn't take it.
Ahead there was an explosion.
They reached a burning Russian tank.
It had rolled over dozens of people,
animals, bedding, household goods,
hay, straw, oats. It was one big mess—
still steaming.
The warmth it gave off felt good.
Later, when she unwrapped Gabi to feed her
the baby was totally quiet.
The woman next to her said:
She's dead.

1945

March

They stand in three rows on the railroad platform
with their suitcases, satchels, and blanket rolls in front of them,
looking left down the track.

The old men,
their hands folded over the handles of their spades,
lean on them.
They are dressed in their finest:
fedoras, caps, suit jackets, ties, polished shoes.
Each is alone in his thoughts,
and if he is afraid
cannot say it to his neighbour.

The young are fifteen, sixteen-years-old.
Their hair is cropped short.
Many look sturdy; some seem frail.
They wear shorts.
One is in Hitler Youth uniform.
He alone looks straight ahead.

Easter

On his last leave in 1943,
my father gave my mother a pistol
and said, "Shoot the children and yourself
when the Russians come."

What does death feel like
I pondered for the next two years.
My friend Hans knew but couldn't tell
because I found him and his family
slumped dead of cyanide poisoning
at their kitchen table.

Shortly after—on an Easter Sunday morning—
we heard the rattling of tank tracks.
The Russians had arrived.
I grabbed the gun from its hiding place
and dropped it down the outhouse toilet
before they kicked in the front door
which was unlocked.

My great-grandparents

White-gowned,
they were bed-ridden
beside each other—
consumed by old age.
They told me stories I've forgotten.
After the Russian tanks clattered up,
we were put into a camp.
What happened to them?

To a Russian prisoner of war

You were kind to me
when I was six.
I thought I'd gone to heaven
the first time you handed me
a hunk of rye bread dipped
in the molasses you boiled
from sugar beets on my
great-grandfather's farm where
you were a slave laborer.
When the Red Army
arrived in our village,
a political commissar arrested you.
Did they execute you as a deserter?

Stoi

I freeze
stare into the gun
barrel pointed
at my face

my body shudders
as he turns

another
puts his hand
on my shoulder
and I know
he misses
his children

It was cold and raining

A man hung from a lamppost.
My mother said, "Don't look."
But I looked anyway.
The wind moved the stiff, dead body
back and forth.

We got on to the back of a truck.
There were benches, and we sat down.
My little brother sat on my mother's lap.
A soldier offered to take me.
Who knows how long we drove.
I fell asleep and woke up
when I realized I'd peed my pants.
The soldier didn't seem to notice.

Finally, we stopped and got off.
There was a big building.
In the ditches lay dead people and animal cadavers.
All around us were horses, cows, even pigs.

It stank.
Inside, we stepped around people with dirty, bloody bandages,
crying children and tired old people.
We were given some soup.
There was no room for us,
so we set out on foot and joined a trek.
The night sky lit up with red and yellow flashes
as we heard the canons fire in the distance.
That night we found shelter in a barn with clean straw.
Still, I didn't sleep well
because I itched from the lice I'd picked up.
In the morning, dandelions and daffodils had appeared.
Life was renewing itself.

Flight

Somehow the bombings were abstract.
You heard the explosions,

you saw the rubble,
you always knew you could be next—

but death was more personal
and chillingly real

when you looked into the still face
of another child now dead

and the blood that stained their coat.
The tragedy of our lives

was that, having gone through
the same experiences together,

we did not recognize each other's
suffering and didn't help each other

better. Instead, we repelled each other.
As I get older

and my skin gets thinner,
these memories are more insistent

and demand their due:
Deal with us or die,

they scream inside my head.
Every spring of my life

I have struggled with whether
I want to live.

Drink and relationship helped me
get through these tough times,

but now I face them alone
and fear for my health and very existence.
       * * *
I sink back into the murky
soup of my unconscious—

saying *not me, not me, can't
catch me*—denying the dead

their once-lived reality, existence,
being and connection to us

now broken by their having
become battered, twisted, frozen

pieces of stiffness that will be
stacked soon, carted off and

buried in a mass grave.
I feel alone in this milling,

shuffling herd
oozing west like a freshly spilt

stain of ink. Beside me,
my mother asks herself, *If I were*

sane, would I scream?
but gives up the thought not

knowing which she is. Best
not to think—move instead

and not collapse. *If I am*
dull, I will not feel.

Alone

There is a place in me where I feel alone.
The memory that comes to mind
is of stumbling behind my mother
on a dirt path in May of 1945.
We are fleeing Russian soldiers.
My mother is carrying my pale,
almost three-year-old brother.
I am six and a half and have diphtheria.
My mother periodically scrapes pus
off my tongue with a spoon
so that I don't choke. I am weak
and can't go on. I want to die.
When I fall, she looks down at me.
And screams, "*NO.*" And curses God.
I look back at her face and realize that,
if I die, she will give up, too.
I must live for her sake.
She pulls me to my feet and we continue.

Raped

I sorrow for you
who was treated brutally

in ways you cannot allow
yourself to remember
except venomously
spewing hatred and rage.
Thank you for not falling
apart until we were safe.

The bargain

A decision was borne
that day. I would keep
you alive so that I
might live. I would take
care of you ... please you.
You would need me,
and I would matter.
We would pull through.

When you stopped weeping,
you smiled at me.
"You are my little man, now."
I was glad to volunteer.

Tackling it

Now the weapons have fallen silent.
People breathe again.
A huge weight has been lifted off them.
They can sleep in peace
and without fear of fighter planes
gunning them when shopping
or working the fields.
Streetlamps glow at dark,
and bicyclists and the few drivers
turn their lights on to see.
A defeated and devastated land
of hungry, homeless people shakes itself

like a mangy dog
and finds its will to begin anew.

That winter is so cold around the world
that Niagara Falls freezes over.
Still, most believe that tomorrow will bring a better world.

Berlin-August, 1945

When I was pushed into
a crater full of glass shards
you carried me
gushing blood
from a deep cut
at the right elbow
to the military hospital
nearby

The army surgeons
consulted—
"Amputation,"
they said
you wept
implored
pleaded

A young surgeon
(who knows: he may have
had a seven-year-old
or perhaps he was moved
by your sad beauty)
took on the gaping wound

When I came to next day
I stumbled from the army cot
into the street
and fainted in your arms

as you returned
from checking on your three-year-old
to tend to your seven-year-old
Today the arm works fine
a huge scar remains
that young American surgeon is surely dead
but his compassion lives on in me

Hiroshima

Warm
sunny
summer
morning
one plane
blinding flash
white light
a roar
black air
swirling wind
silence
cries
for help
fire
panic
faces
blister
swell
skin
hanging
from arms
moans
stench
everything
turned
into
solitary
nothingness
akirame

one grave
for the bodies
none
for the souls
God's power
now
in the hands
of man

The rubble women
who were former fellow-travelers
stand in long rows
on the mountainous ruins
filling pails with broken bricks,
passing them from hand to hand
down to the street.
If you take their picture
or jeer them,
they stick their tongues out at you.
Are they the heroines this age craves—
next to the black-market profiteers?

My hero

My hero was Robin Hood and I, too,
took from the rich to give to the poor.
My mother's bottom line was, "Whatever you do,
don't get caught because I'll have to
punish you for that." I was only caught
once, stealing flowers for Mother's Day.

The cat

I was a black panther.
I prowled during the day
and hunted at night.

My prey were the slats of fences,
tomato stakes, timber scraps from ruins,
broken furniture, dead branches.
Every night, as people prepared for bed,
I silently passed their windows
with my bounty of firewood.

As the old world collapsed

my mother and all those who no longer grieved
danced the boogie-woogie with the "Amis"
out of joy of survival, out of a lust for life.
The war still echoed, and death was yet so near.

My schoolmates

They were defusing a bomb
to sell for scrap metal.
It exploded.
Our school closed for the funeral.
A long column of us walked
behind the coffins to the graveyard.
As the boxes disappeared into the ground,
we avoided each other's eyes.
It could have been us.

My grandmother

was a comet
that streaked
across the night sky
of my young life
before she gassed
herself
one evening.
For two weeks
I loved her
as one

who is starved
for love
does.
Then there she lay in a dim room.
She looked as though she was asleep.
But very pale, waxen, foreign—
already far away.
She wore a paper nightgown
and was covered by a paper sheet.
Her hands were folded over her stomach
and held some cornflowers.
I felt sick.

At her funeral,
as the coffin
was lowered
into the ground,
I vowed
never to love,
never to suffer
such a loss,
and never to
attend another funeral
again.

My fear

The mother
of the boy
across the street
hanged herself
last night.
This morning
he found her
dangling
by the front window.
My friend Willi says
the boy is going
to an orphanage.

1946

Winter

Again, I hear
the clatter of his push-cart.
His cheeks are hollow
and his sunken eyes rarely stray
from the wooden box
which shields a baby
or a grandmother who
froze or starved to death
last night. The ground
is stone-hard with frost.
Willi says nobody digs graves
in this weather.
No matter what,
I remembered.
With my eyes closed, I saw.
With my body tensed, I shuddered.
What I tried to forget, I recalled.
Then the migraine gripped me,
and my head became a throbbing mass of pain.
Darkness relieved it.
That day I left my body,
floated to the ceiling, and found relief
looking down on myself.

When God's face was hidden
they deliberately killed
6 million Jews from all over Europe
5 million Russian civilians
2 million Polish civilians
1 million gypsies and supposedly insane or incurable sick Germans
8 million others of "inferior stock"

There were 15 000 concentration camps in Nazi-occupied Europe, an additional 25 000 slave labour camps, as well as peripatetic killer battalions. 3 600 women worked as guards in the concentration camps.

This past was never expunged. Only 60 of the women guards were charged with crimes in the first five years after the war. The vast majority of Nazis were never prosecuted. In fact, most found employment rebuilding Germany as government officials, police, lawyers, judges, teachers, and businessmen. With their snouts in the troughs of reconstruction, these perpetrators had each other's backs.

The owners of BMW, Daimler-Benz, Porsche, Volkswagen, Allianz, Krupp, Oetker, and so on, who supplied the weapons and material to fight this conflict profited mightily and got off lightly with American connivance. Once again, humanity had failed.

When I was seven
my mother taught me to read
because there were no schools.
My father, who had disappeared in Russia,
left behind a library.
In it I found a book by Ovid
titled *The Art of Love.*
It was the first book I tried to read on my own.
To my disappointment, it did not explain
what the American soldiers were doing
with their German girlfriends behind the
condom-festooned bushes in our park.

Exterminations

I didn't know.
They deserved it.
I was helpless.
I didn't do it.
It's in the past.

Yet these were crimes:
so enormous, so monstrous,
they will be with us forever.
Unmoved, they talk about
the good old days.

You cannot argue
with prejudice,
or excuses,
or biology.

Marked

It is endlessly here:
the secret evil
that makes you pretend,
"I didn't know."
Or rationalize,
"There was a war on."
Or excuse yourself,
"I'm not a martyr."
But you still feel guilt—
impotently, unresolved,
confusing culpability.
The past is always now
as you witness the grinding loneliness
of the survivor whose death
was interrupted by chance.

Silence

If you think of yourself as a victim,
you can avoid responsibility
for the unthinkable that was done
in your name.
And so the Holocaust,
the extermination camps,
the memories of deported neighbours,
were hushed up during the years
of struggle after the war.

The taboo

Have the right attitude.
Play it safe.
Don't argue. Don't question.
Be pleasant. Pretend.
And don't sully our family
by asking questions your parents
don't want to answer.
What's the big fuss, anyway?
People were only doing
what they'd been ordered to do.

There are reasons

why some become monsters.
They hate.
We can understand
but must not excuse.
I, who was born too late
to do harm, cannot escape
where I come from
and what was done by my people.
I am forever a child of the mist,
but I always look at myself
and atone with care.
I am not Sisyphus.

In locum patris

My mother hung a sign
over our kitchen table
whose message she drummed
into me, "Knowledge is power,
and power is money."
What she could not give me
was a father's inner authority
and strength.

Contentment

I felt genuinely happy
the afternoon you and I
sat in the living room—
you reading on the couch
and I sitting on the rug
playing with my wooden blocks.
Sunlight poured in through the window;
the black cherry tree was in full blossom
and leaned into the balcony.
The radio played classical music.
There was no war, no fear—
only peace.

Years later when I had become a man,
my wife and I sat kitty-corner
in our living room reading.
It was a rare luxury.
I looked at her absorbed in her book
and felt a wave of gratitude and joy
coursing through me.

Homecoming

He looked scruffy, emaciated and lame,
a scarecrow dressed in a greatcoat and cap
staring up at her window.
Then there was a knock on the door,
and he stood there holding his discharge papers
as if to tell her who he was.
Suddenly, her son declared, "That's Dad."
For months afterwards, he was there but not there
and behaved strangely—at times lifeless, hollow and mute;
at others bad-tempered, bitter and angry
that his wife and children managed so well without him.
And as he growled and cursed,
they drifted apart and he became pitied and feared.
When he took the last cube of sugar
from the pantry and said it must have been one of the children,
she'd had enough.

Religion

I only believed in rational things.
So, I was kicked out of confirmation class
for questioning the literal truth
of the Virgin Birth and of the Resurrection
and asking why slaves who believed
in Jesus were worked to death.
Now I was a heathen and Suzie,
the girl I had a crush on, worried
I might not be admitted to Heaven.
We debated this nightly--me sitting
in the tree outside her window
and she leaning on the sill.
Then I knew the promise of an after-life
had been a bribe to keep me in the fold.
Looking back, I was a Buddhist
before my time. Is Christianity a theology
of convenience for the deserving?

Or, could it again be the counterculture
it was in its beginnings?

1948 - June 21

Yesterday the stores were empty.
Today there is food and clothing
on the shelves, and people
are busy spending the
forty Deutsche Marks
which currency reform has given them.
And I no longer have to smuggle
bread and beet sugar out of East Berlin.
I will miss skipping school,
buying water ice cream, and
visiting the Pergamon Museum.

A year of grace

When in 1948 the Soviet Union cut off road access to Berlin in order
to starve out the city, two families in Sweden offered to take in my
brother and me. Our journey, on our own, took four days.
I stayed with a middle-aged couple whom I ended up calling Tante
Anna and Onkel Sven. On the first night, I scouted their place and
stole the money from the milk box. They were so kind to me at
breakfast that I apologized and returned the coins. My year with them
was a turning point in my life. I was cared for instead of being a
caretaker. I was allowed to be a child. I began to feel more than fear
and anger. I was valued for myself.

To my mother

You were abandoned and abused
as a child—your heart was broken—
yet you repeated the past.

When I was seven, our roles changed.
You told me I was your little man now.
You said you loved me,
yet I felt hurt and afraid.
Something was wrong.

Some days the darkness lifted.
There was order, calm, even joy.
The world was good.
Then the storm returned,
and I feared and hated you again.

I needed to keep you alive
so that I might live, too.
I worked hard to lighten your burden
and please you.
I watched you closely when you thought of suicide.
I sat with you during your rages and tears
and felt your fear and your emptiness.
After a time, I didn't know where you ended and I began.
Your needs consumed all,
filled the room—
wired me to be compliant, inauthentic, on guard,
trying to understand the unfathomable.
And my father was gone—lost, dead?
Grieving him meant betraying you,
so I kept my mouth shut.

Later, in my dreams I searched for a door
that leads to myself.
Instead, it happened that I opened
a window to the wind
and flew out myself.
I now had a life of my own
but still felt guilty.

Who was he?

He only spoke one sentence
I remember.

I went to meet him at the train station
when he returned from Siberia in 1951.
"Where's your mother?"
was all this gaunt stranger said.

A moment later, after I gave him her note,
he was furious with me
and then vanished once more.
I never saw him again.
That's how my mother wanted it.

Years later, I woke up one night
longing for him and wept.

Thank you

for giving me life
for loving me
even if absent-mindedly
and in spite of your pain
thank you too
for not killing yourself
when life was bleak
and cheap
thank you
for insisting I live
when I wanted to die
thank you
for selling your body
so that I might eat
thank you
for teaching me to read
and to love books
thank you
for the Sunday mornings
when you made
sharing an egg and a bun
into a feast

Adolescence

My life changed dramatically when my mother married again in 1952 when I was fourteen. She was thirty-eight, fresh out of an abusive relationship, felt unworthy, and longed for security and an end to struggling. It was slim pickings because men were scarce. A year later we emigrated to Canada and ended up in Niagara Falls.

My stepfather resented having stepchildren—in particular, I was a competitor to him. At the same time, I lost the close, unhealthy relationship with my mother in which I was her partner and support.

I still felt protective of my mother as she was hurt by Walter's neglect, his affairs, and his alcoholism.

Once a week, usually on a Saturday night, my mother screamed. Her words were vile. I still hated her for this. But I closed the windows and sat with her. Walter went to the basement and drank. My brother stayed in his room. That much rageful screaming does something to your brain. I go blank and numb at the memory of it.

The rest of the week I walked a tightrope and tried to please and appease both of them with helpful behavior, giving them my earnings, and performing well at school, in athletics, and other extracurricular activities.

In the end, I was desperate and stuck—silently furious with both, not talking to them, running away, and then smoking and drinking at their instigation. I began to wish I was dead.

1954 Niagara Falls

I am grateful for the memory
of a sunny Saturday morning
when I was sixteen.
For a few hours
I was a normal teenager
playing basketball with other boys.
I was so happy
I could smell the sunshine,
and everything felt right
with the world for that moment.

A last hope

I saw the school counsellor
today about my family life.
He told me to pray
and ask God for help.
I've been doing this for years
although last night I told God
our arrangement was not working
and signed off with him
to go it alone from now on.

If God simply is—
unmoved;
and we who respond
to suffering and inequity
with care are not—
then why do we need Him?

The mystery may vanish,
and the sacred be elusive,
but the holy longing remains.

There is no time —
each moment is eternal
filled with pain
ever to be repeated.
I sink to unknown depths
am naked of all defenses
submersed in self.
Will I ever rediscover
reverence for life,
find meaning, joy, kindness,
caring, even love?
Over the years
I have persuaded myself
that I don't need
what I wasn't given.
At school, I have a chip
on my shoulder telling
everyone to stay away.

Slow down
my head throbs
with the intensity
of so much motion
noise light
never forgetting
I feel dissonant
overloaded
crazy want out
away
all is spinning
I am collapsing
give me order
predictability
certainty calm
allow my rituals
before I implode
or rage

My parents

I busted a gut,
stood on my head
and spit nickels
to please you.
It didn't get me
what you couldn't give
(and hadn't gotten yourselves),
nor did I make you
happier.

Seventeen

When I ran away from home
to a hell-hole called Seaton House
in Toronto and came back a week later,
you were both silent.
When I tore up the front lawn
with my '36 Ford Coupe
and passed out drunk on the steps,
neither of you said anything.
Acknowledging my pain would have
meant admitting to yours.
You were not ready, then or later,
and I'm sad I never got to know you.

Eighteen

When I turned eighteen
I was initiated into manhood.
My parents gave me
the 'phone number of a prostitute,
twenty dollars to pay her,
a bottle of brandy,
and a carton of cigarettes.
I threw away the first

and kept the rest.
Since they had not taught me
to be an adult
nor helped me to know my strengths,
the old in me would not die
and the new could not be born.
Still tied and obligated
and without their permission to separate,
I continued to feel undeserving
of love and acceptance and sought belonging
through caretaking and achievements.

The Fifties

My parents thought
they could break my will,
like their parents before them.
The best they could do
was damage it.

I chose not to have children.

Somewhere
there's a locked drawer
that holds my grief
I've forgotten where
I put the key.

2

In the dark wood

What we don't let out traps us.
We think, No one else feels this way,
I must be crazy. So, we don't say anything.
And we become enveloped by a deep loneliness,
not knowing where our feelings come from or what to do with them.
Why do I feel this way?
—Sabrina Ward Harrison

As an adolescent
I became an ascetic
and made a virtue
of my deprivation
of intimate connection.

It may be convenient, but...
it is dishonest to stay
when you have already left.
It is also dishonest to allow
another, who has already left, to stay.

Albert Einstein observed,
"The most important decision we make
is whether we believe we live
in a friendly or hostile universe."
I am ambivalent, even though I am now
out of immediate harm's way.

The wasp

The wasp flying outside my window
becomes entangled in a spider's web.
The wasp twists,
turns and struggles.
Suddenly, the spider darts at the wasp.
The web bounces.
The wasp frees itself—
or is it freed?
And flies away.
The spider retreats to the edge.

A spider just unfettered a wasp
and each goes on as before,
flying, waiting ....

Why I drink

When I ask my soul
what it needs
it answers
a connection of the heart
the kind where
you entrust the other
with your life
yet
in the presence of
my sense of obliteration
when dying feels real
and I could
make it happen
I drink

If

I were free of old fears
I would not lie to myself
to quiet the pain
of life's betrayals
but would ask
honestly, "What do I avoid
that You ask of me?"

On being 18 or 24 or 30 and male without a father

I crammed
facts
in order to have
a power
I did not feel

Meeting an idol

I'd been good at track and field—sprints, javelin, discus. Good enough to be made captain of the junior team in Grade 10.

Johnny Long was our coach. He worked us hard and the year I was captain, I won first place in the regional 100- and 220-yard dashes and second in the 440 and the javelin throw.

Years later, I was selling textbooks to the Ministry of Education. As I walked to my appointment, I saw Johnny Long, now an official, more wrinkled, but absolutely still like my idol of yesterday.

"Mr. Long," I started, still hoping for the pat on the back he'd never given me.

He didn't recognize me.

"Greg Sass. Stamford Collegiate. I was on your track and football teams."

"Oh, yes," he looked at me over his reading glasses. "Hope you're doing well." And he walked on.

The shrine my parents built to me
stood only for as long as I met
their expectations.
When I left and took my past with me,
the art I had created for them,
my childhood photos, too,
were torn and burnt.
As they tried to murder my soul,
I grieved and was reborn.
My brother, who replaced me as their champion,
stayed in the fold and with his heart's agenda
not served, died young of brain cancer.

Two old people now held each other hostage,

and when *he* died, *she* refused him
a public notice, a coffin, a visitation,
a funeral, and a marker.
And never spoke of him again.
I scattered his ashes in the Atlantic
and thanked him for the one thing
he did well—teaching me to drive.

I am unkind for there was more ....
When I shot a starling,
his anger taught me
it is wrong to kill wantonly.
He gave me his track shoes
with which I raced.
He gave me his French beret
with which I stood out.
He bought and fixed up
the first cars I drove.
And he cried in front of me
when his mother died.
The tension between us
did not allow for more—
more often.

Legacy

They were like two
little children
disguised
as my parents,
terrifyingly needy
as well as demanding.
And I felt responsible for them.

Now I shrink
every time an institution
makes a personal demand on me.
I can give money
but no longer my self.

I have no friends,
no lover,
no children—
I cannot depend
or be depended upon.
I am a stranger to myself.

Women

I have not known
what is good for me,
because I have been more
concerned with
what is good for them.

Or so I thought.

Looking for two to see one

I asked two doctors for help this year.
One told me to shape up.
The other offered me Valium.
I then found a commune
where at least I live with others.
Here I have started to remember
and can't stop talking.

Vietnam

"We had to destroy it
to save it.
What the fuck
were we doing there?"

Coming back

Our life begins twice: the day we are born
and the day we accept the radical existential fact
that our life, for all its delimiting factors,
is essentially ours to choose.
—James Hollis

I dreamt

about three people
whose needs I had
to meet before
I was allowed to
leave them.

Two were vague,
maybe male.
The third was a sick
woman whose body
was disfigured by sores.

I touched her feet and
salved the wounds there
and then walked out
into my own future.

You

can't
forgive
what
you
don't understand

A grief transformed

One day
I turned a corner
as I remembered
a treasured moment
with gratitude
instead of sadness

God

God is that which
illuminates my life
and the mystery
that transforms me
the more I am willing.
I have lost the god
who stopped protecting me
when I was young.
Sometimes I still wish
for certainty and unconditional
love.

Dear brother,

When you were dying, you told me that you felt I had always gotten more than you did in our family. You were not angry, but once again— and now for the last time —our hearts chilled and our souls starved. Soon after you lapsed into a coma, and we never did sort this out.

I remember you as a delicate, quiet, soulful child. You were ethereal—almost not of this world. I often looked after you but, in retrospect, it feels as though you were on the sidelines watching while our mother and I took care of our needs and were thus connected.

When you were five and still malnourished and unwell, you were sent to live with a family on Lake Constance in Switzerland. When you came back, I picked you up. You had something black, sticky, and sweet-smelling in your hand that you wanted me to have. It was a banana you said. You had saved it for me even though it was part of the lunch for your journey.

Six years later, with my first paycheque from my first summer job, I bought you your first bicycle.

We looked after one another, and our acts of love and care gave meaning to hardship and helped us survive hunger, cold, fear, and danger. There were Sundays in those days when things were almost right with the world. Our mother would send me out to buy one egg, one bun, and a dab of butter. We divided these into three portions and had a feast sitting in our sun-drenched living room while the black cherry tree, in blossom or in fruit, leaned into our balcony. And the radio played light opera and classical music.

You were so ready for a real father when our mother married again and you were eight. Unfortunately, you suffered much verbal abuse as you sought to befriend your stepfather. But you persisted, and the two of you spent many hours under the hoods of cars after we came to Canada. In the process, you became a doer—a young man who throve on practical problems and tasks and eventually learned how to fix almost anything.

When you were nineteen—it's still incredible that the school board put you into grade one at the age of eleven—you joined me in Toronto and finished high school there. Unfortunately, you'd been called "stupid" by our stepfather too often and found it difficult to persist in higher education. I was glad we lived together for those one and a half years. I introduced you to my friends, the cultural scene in Toronto, and helped you into adulthood—help that I wish I had had.

But you, like me, were a novice to feelings, relationships, love, and maturity. Like me at age twenty-one, you married the first woman who wanted you. It was a rocky beginning. At your engagement, our mother and her mother yelled at each other, each claiming that the other was socially inferior.

While our mother (abetted by her husband) pushed your wife and her family away, they also pulled you closer to themselves and made you responsible for their needs. At the very same moment, I had decided that I would no longer be at our parents' beck and call or make right what was dysfunctional between them. Without a word being said, you took on my role. You were now the "good son," and I became the "bad" one. Of course, it was all conditional—as always. I wondered if I had sacrificed you, so that I could escape.

Our stepfather soon paid me back for my alleged abandonment of the family. In an attempt to create a better relationship among us, you invited our mother, stepfather, and me to spend Christmas Eve the next year at your and your wife's place. Our stepfather was soon drunk and accused me of reneging on the oath of loyalty to the family he had made us swear when we arrived in Canada. He ordered me to take the oath again in front of everyone. When I remained silent, he threw me to the floor, pushed my face into the carpet, and forced me to repeat the oath. No one moved. No one said a word then or immediately afterwards. Nor was it ever mentioned again during the rest of our lives. We lived in silence, except when he was drunk or our mother was screaming.

And yet, you and I remained close. Now you were often the capable one, and you were generous of yourself. One incident says it all. I blew the engine of my sports car while in Gaspé one summer. When I phoned you for advice on whether to salvage the car, you rented a flatbed, drove 900 miles to meet me, and carried the little car in the back of your truck to Toronto.

We spent time together in your workshop where you taught me to weld. And you, in turn, came to my place every week to participate in a seminar I was running on educational reform.

Gradually, as you realized that I was not returning to the fold, we drifted apart. I sensed that you were telling your wife and our parents things that I thought I had said to you in confidence. I felt you were doing this to diminish me, and I was disappointed.

I was also concerned for you. You were the last of that breed of men who rose through the ranks without the benefit of higher education but instead by dint of native intelligence and talent, lots of hands-on experience, and enormous raw energy. And you were decent. When, after your death, I spoke to some of the two hundred people who worked for you, they praised you for your fairness and humanity, your accessibility, and your dedication to your work. Your routine was to rise at 5 a.m. daily and put in full days as a manager, involved parent, householder, helpful neighbour, scoutmaster, and caregiver to our parents. The cost was that you became flabby, pre-diabetic, depressed, and subject to undiagnosed ailments. You put yourself last.

At age fifty-two, you were diagnosed with brain cancer. You were brave, strong, uncomplaining, worked hard at recovery, and became more spiritual and loving.

I was out of work the spring when you were admitted to palliative care. I sat by your bedside daily and wrote down your caring and passionate outpourings about everyone you loved—your wife and children, your in-laws, your children's friends, your neighbours and friends, your co-workers, the animals. You asked me to deliver these messages at your funeral. You then planned the menu for the reception after the funeral and discussed it with the cook.

You stayed in character. After wasting away from 225 pounds to 120 pounds and having been paralyzed for almost two weeks, you said to me, "This has been a wonderfully exciting if sometimes frightening experience. Even having my head scratched feels terrific."

Your innocence, your sense of wonder, your selflessness, and your goodness of heart stay with me.

Sometimes

Sometimes there is silence
and fear grips my heart
as I walk alone.
Then I am the motherless child—
desolate, worthless, and abandoned,
and wish I were dead.
"What is wrong with me, and what have I done
to be given this?" I ask.
"Face me," is the reply,
"and become at one with what you find."
Prayer is contemplation of the sacred.

The void

Unlike depression,
the void waits for me
behind a trap door
that falls open
beneath my feet.
I stare into the abyss
and shudder.

Ending slow suicide

Today
an angel crossed my path.
She saw in me
what I had forgotten
about myself and said,
"You are too good
to hurt yourself like this."
Every day now is a disaster
full of chaos, guilt,
self-hatred, pain.

For twenty-nine years I hadn't wanted to live
until this kind lover said I was worthwhile.
Now was the first time I felt cared for.
It made me value myself,
and I began to flower.
I thank that woman
and regret I didn't do the same for her.
Only later did I realize
how courageously she lived with MS.
I have since helped others to want to live.

Regna

I
am
the
seed bearer
of
many
of
my
problems
and
the
person
I
hurt
most
in
this
life
is
me

My life begins for the second time

Finally, I was ready. An alcoholic acquaintance developed Korsakoff Syndrome and killed himself. This shook me, and in 1985 I quit drinking and smoking and stepped back from the void. With that I stopped pretending that I was or had to be "somebody." I was reduced to being myself which, without its pretensions, wasn't much. But I now knew what it's like to be raw, human; to be stripped-to-the-bone poor, yet feel rich in spirit; and to be deeply moved by the moon setting as the sun was rising over Lake Ontario. I had found the "me" I lost when young. I cleaned toilets at night and my soul during the day. And it was a joy to be alive starting over again at age forty-six, no longer afraid of letting life happen. I met my second wife, Lynda, the following year.

God grant me the strength

to be my own person
and live my own life,
no longer hiding behind
niceness, conformity,
and self-promotion.

Dawn

As the sky explodes
with light and colour,
I give thanks
and wish my fellow beings well.
It is wondrous to be alive.

Woodend

two stone pillars
an iron gate half-open
beyond
a back door
framed in white clapboard
an abandoned garden
overgrown with weeds
sunny and shaded by trees
my step-grandson says
ask God if we can rent a room here

On my mother's death at ninety

When I attended to my mother's estate,
I found a book I had written and dedicated to her.
The dedication page with my inscription
had been ripped out.
Although it hurts that I ceased to be
even a duty-bound-good-enough-son,

I know that she did not choose her terror
of abandonment and the wildness it brought on.
She was sometimes heroic
and often did the best she could,
but I grieve her later life which was a desert.

Manhood is a struggle

When I was a child, there was a stigma attached to being fatherless. It often meant you were poor, on government assistance, and that your mother did things that people looked down on.

When I became an adolescent, I sought out men—on construction gangs, in sports, and in the comradeship and shared dangers of soldiering.

Still, I was sensitive and therefore averse to senseless violence. I challenged myself but resisted being pushed around or shamed into being macho. I was often lonely as a result and found myself on the side of the underdog and the outsider.

Later, I spent many years numbed and anesthetized, lost to myself and often swamped by old traumas striving for position, status, more money. These were mostly all I had to define me and hopefully prove my manhood. Like the monkey with his hand in the trap, I could not let go of these power symbols and be free.

Finally, I gave all that up and learnt to feel as well as think. I entered life and took responsibility for myself. In AA, I bonded more safely with men than I had before. I was fortunate to find a father surrogate in my sponsor. I was no longer an impostor but knew I belonged in the company of men.

Am I still angry at what once was? *No.* I have played with fire and done enough to hurt myself. Now I sorrow for those who as yet don't know better and value my own good fortune.

You stifled a scream

I did not notice.
Eventually, even you
no longer heard yourself.
Only your body remembered,
without knowing that fear
has a name.

The harmony you desire
is contradicted by the war
the cells in your body
wage on each other
regardless of your survival
or theirs.

Please stop picking at the scab
that covers the memory of losing
the job you loved.
I fear this will kill you.

Sacred passage

(by Lynda Rose)

Love is our true destiny.
We do not find the meaning of life by ourselves alone—
we find it with another.
—Thomas Merton

From Lynda's journal—June 2006

I

The main item on my *To Do* list for today is to find an upholsterer for the chairs and sofa.

Did the cancer come to motivate me to develop my mind and spirituality? Or, will we someday see cancer as a virus and something easily dealt with?

Words from a hymn come to me, "Precious Lord Take My Hand...."

What kind of message should I leave Greg to find after I die? Telephone? Letter?

Does planning for my death mean I don't have enough will to heal myself and live? Maybe ....

Should I plan only for living to increase my communication to healing? Should I stay only in Now to enjoy this moment which I know I have? I keep going in circles and coming back to NOW. It's all we have to enjoy.

II

This belief that bad things will happen to me has been part of me since my infancy. I believed it as a child. Nobody wanted me for a friend. If they did, either we'd move or they'd change their mind. As a child I always believed there was a secret to being accepted, liked, and loved, and I didn't know it. Without that secret, I would fail or lose.

Two years ago, this belief surfaced very clearly and strongly when I realized I wasn't getting the promotion I'd applied for. Other people said I was worrying needlessly, but I was very scared. When I failed to get the position because the other woman had more seniority, I again felt that the cards of life were stacked against me. No matter how good I was at my work, I wouldn't have been able to win.

I had to resign myself to losing this job that I'd already been doing for two years and that I believed I was an ideal fit for. I decided to leave all of my work in perfect order and to be a gracious loser. This I did, but I lost all interest in my career. I think I was depressed and ashamed somehow.

III

My abdomen is crampy. Could I have another obstruction? The CT scan would have shown that. Fear is preying on me again.

If I have metastases, how will I react? I expect to continue the inner work I've started. As I wait, this work feels more important than the results of the MRI.

How will I talk to my daughters next weekend?

***

I had lunch with a co-worker yesterday. I don't know her well. She surprised me by saying that I'm a role model for her and an important person in her life.

I wish I hadn't retold my history of life with my ex-husband. I could have been a better listener. I wish, too, I'd acknowledged and thanked her for telling me that I mattered to her.

However, I realized that my entire life has been a struggle and that I haven't had much peace.

**

I'm affirming that healing is my number one priority. I'm afraid to tell my daughters about the cancer. Thank God for Greg's wisdom and support and my sisters for listening.

IV

Death means leaving and loss. It reminds me of the helplessness and resignation I felt as a child whenever we moved. How does this deep pattern affect my cancer and my healing?

I have two contradictory beliefs about myself. On the one hand, I'm a good, capable, kind person who is able to handle and resolve problems. On the other hand, bad things happen to me. It's not fair, but I'm resigned to accepting them with good grace. There's nothing I can do to stop those bad things (losses) from happening. Somehow, they are my lot in life. There's a secret to having happiness, but I don't know it even though I have searched diligently.

This second, early, strong belief lurks below my consciousness always—making me feel sad and powerless and also guilty for having these bad things happen to me, and for not being happy and energized.

V

Yesterday we hiked, and Greg took my picture. I thought, "I may not do this next June. I may be dead or dying."

I am sad to leave such a beautiful world and Greg. Everything in my life is perfect, except for this cancer.

I must be fooling myself, or I wouldn't have cancer again. But how can I change something when I don't know what it is that's wrong. I have changed everything I know about.

Maybe it's my time to die. I don't want to die and leave all the good things in my life. I want to stay alive, and I'm going to fight to do it.

But how? I don't even know for sure I have metastases. Maybe the radiologist was premature. I'm glad I have this time before June 15 before I know what the MRI shows.

VI

Greg did some trauma-reduction work with me this morning. I was afraid to face any of my negative beliefs. I've been fending them off but maybe I have to work through them. This will be a lot of work and I have a lot of fears.

When I was crying, Greg remained calm. How does he do it? Perhaps he was wearing his "counsellor's hat" —but even so I was very impressed. He's an excellent therapist. His sense of timing is right on. I'm very blessed to have him as my husband.

***

I said I wouldn't but I'm thinking about the future. Me sick or dying or dead. How will Greg cope? How do I prepare for this—leaving my life and my world, leaving Greg?

VII

Greg and I do some more trauma-reduction work. The fears and negative beliefs that I identify are: I'm afraid that I don't have some unknown, innate quality that is essential to do my spiritual work successfully. I just don't know the "trick." Also, if I had done this work successfully after breast cancer, I wouldn't be here again. And, finally, I'm afraid that I won't be able to complete this work in time to heal myself before I die.

My throat is tight. I find it hard to speak, and I cry a lot as I describe these fears to Greg. Feelings of failure, anticipatory loss, lack of control, helplessness, hopelessness, loneliness, and abandonment pour out of me.

And then, I believe in myself again.

I have already been successful with a lot of healing work when I had breast cancer, and I'll find what I need to get through this level of healing, too.

Healing myself is a goal. Spiritual work is a daily practice, slowly revealing small insights that will gradually heal my spirit and my body. It's a daily journey of many minute discernments, each an effort to untangle but such a relief and lightness when accomplished. Sometimes there's a surprise; sometimes it's reworking an old, familiar theme. I can't control—and there's no guarantee—that I'll achieve my goal of body healing, but I can re-commit myself to daily practice and feel positive about it.

VIII

Greg's mother died six months ago, and our work of caring for children, grandchildren, and aging parents was coming to an end. Greg and I would have time for ourselves soon, but then I got colon cancer.

I have handled this cancer with a sort of calm and the old sense of resignation, sadness, anticipatory grieving, low energy, and fatigue.

Again, I'm betting against myself emotionally, even though I fight on the surface. Again, I'm afraid that I won't be able to find the "secret" to staying alive and enjoying my life with Greg. Underneath I'm already preparing to die as per my old belief that bad things happen to me. Compliance with God's will is only a variation on this theme.

I want to change this belief. For starters I am going to refuse to plan for dying; and refuse to worry about Greg's grief.

IX

I am very sad and frightened since my last appointment with Dr. G. There is the increased reality of more and inoperable liver and lung metastases and possible others (what is the lump on my right upper abdomen they found two days ago?).

At lunch with J., I cried and said I felt like a battle is going on inside me between my negative thoughts of fear, despair, and grief and my will and hope to live. I feel overwhelmed by negativity. It's like being on a mystic journey or vision quest where the hero must fight internal demons as well as external ones. It reminds me of Ransom in C.S. Lewis' *Voyage to Venus* where he had to deal with Galom over and over and over.

X

I appreciate three things:
   My relationship with Greg is more intimate. Our time together is of high quality. We are real "kindred spirits."

I am able to focus on healing mind and spirit which is what I always wanted to do but was distracted by life from doing. And I now have the time for this work.

Greg and I walk in nature and cherish this beautiful world.

XI

I ask joy and peace to come into me. It's okay to feel pain. My job now is healing. Am I doing or being? Productive or intrinsically valuable? I accept this moment as if I had chosen it.

***

My belly sticks out when I sit and relax. Is it full of pressure from a swollen liver (metastases)? Who knows? We'll see.

***

I can share anything with Greg and my sisters. And I have four very supportive friends.

***

Does having cancer oblige me to make changes in my life? What kinds of changes? What would be helpful to fight the cancer?

***

I don't want to be sad, scared, and grieving and waste the time I do have. Sometimes I feel the stress in my chest and I cry. I fear what's ahead for me, and I fear what's ahead for Greg. And I'm angry. It's not fair. And I'm embarrassed about my emotional displays and making it harder for Greg to stay in control.

Since I was a child, I have felt an overwhelming sense of loss and grief and a helplessness to prevent it. I felt this way when Mom was dying too.

XII

I feel huge gratitude to God for relief of fear, grief, and negative thinking. My left brain and ego are still unbelieving, but there has been a real shift. Thank you, God, for these minutes of peace.

***

In my group, we talked about Ram Dass's observation: "When we practice dying, we are learning to identify less with Ego and more with

Soul." And death's inevitability. A lot of us were crying. Greg told his group about me—I'm glad he'll have support from them.

***

My liver area feels swollen. Will this pressure become pain? What if the metastases are growing faster and I die soon? I need to finish up my projects so Greg is left without extra work.

***

Today I felt wonderful—not sure why. This transformational journey is very exciting because I have always wanted to find out about the spirit-connected self inside me and join with her. I feel like I've started on an adventure.

***

I have conflicting ideas about healing. Do I focus only on Now and on positive thoughts, feelings, and healthier responses to life? Or do I also pay attention to and express feelings that include negative ones?

XIII

I hear Greg move around. I love him. What if I die? I don't want to think that. It makes me cry.

The weather is beautiful. Time flies lately. Is it because it's limited?

My healing is most important now. Our life these days revolves around me and my cancer and my healing. Does Greg resent this? I asked him. He said, "Not in the least. This is what's in front of us right now." I felt relieved.

XIV

I lived the story and fiction of Princess Valiant. I was good, moral, intelligent, and determined. I was a victim, not a perpetrator. I was a heroine and fought for righteous causes on behalf of others and myself. I survived but at a great— especially emotional—cost. I focused intensively on problems and solutions but not enough on my own peace, well-being, and happiness.

A truer story would be me as a peaceful, loved, valued, joyful, beautiful, grateful child of God.

XV

I saw B. for cranio-sacral therapy today. She asked me if I considered my life to be a spiritual experience. Her cat snuggled up to me, and said that the cat had never done this before with a client.

Tomorrow morning I will see Dr. G. to find out the results of my liver MRI.

***

Greg is doing a lot of work researching alternative healing modalities. Right now he's looking into Traditional Chinese Medicine—acupuncture, herbs, and concoctions that seem vile. Thinking of getting involved in this scares me.

XVI

I skipped practice because I feel so bad. I've felt afraid and sad and even angry (for the first time) since seeing Dr. G. three days ago. I've done a lot of crying and I'm exhausted. So I sleep in the mornings and go for walks with Greg in the evenings.

I feel as if I've let myself down. The old critical thoughts about not doing what I need to do well enough and being disciplined enough are back. It's an old pattern, and it gets worse when I'm under stress. But I'm afraid of dying if I don't do this right. I don't want to die—not for myself and not for Greg.

So I'll try to watch and control my thoughts better and try to stay "on track."

***

I wonder if I should find a therapist and spend more time with friends. I don't want to feel alone.

XVII

We had planned to walk after supper but income tax took much longer and then Greg was too tired and so I went out alone at ten.

The evening was warm and fragrant and wonderful. I was happy to be out walking in this incredibly gorgeous weather and lushness of June. I did have a few fearful thoughts, but they had no power against this incredible evening.

And then on the way home, which is downhill, I felt like running. And so I ran. I could hardly believe I was running—like in my visualization of my "ideal self." I didn't run far but it felt so easy, so effortless almost. I was light and surprised and very happy. I don't think I have wanted to run since I left British Columbia when I was twelve. What an incredible experience and treasure!

**

I'm glad I made the effort to go out and walk and run last night. I love walking at night. The air is fragrant with lilacs and pansies and soft and warm on my skin. A slight breeze cools my nostrils. I feel free and light and strong and whole. This is heaven on earth.

XVIII

In my life, I always set out plans for myself—things I should do or must do. And when I felt too tired to do them, I just told myself, "I have enough energy to do what I have to do," and kept on going. I didn't pay attention to my tired body nor was I ever able to discover why I was always so tired.

Right now, when I'm tired, I don't say that anymore. But I could spend a few minutes thinking about why I might be so tired. Is it because I need more rest, or is it because my unhealed mind has set up the wrong plans to save itself again? And my fatigue is a signal of something being wrong. Perhaps all the plans my mind makes are based on illusions—and they're all wrong.

**

Right now I feel anxious about the healing plans for my cancer. I believed that spiritual work was all I needed. Yet Greg believes I should be doing more and is still doing a lot of research to discover what the "more" may be. By pleasing him, am I undermining my belief that the spiritual work is enough on its own? I don't think so. There are many ways to heal because people are so different. If spiritual work was the only way, then anyone else who wasn't aware of it would die—and that's not true.

I hope that by becoming more loving and peaceful, my body will heal itself. I hope to transform my anxious, controlling ego-self into a more accepting holy-self.

***

My body and the little world I inhabit will disappear when I die. My apartment will not be the way I have organized it. My plants will not be the way I've arranged and cared for them. Greg's life will be dramatically different. My children's and grandchildren's lives will go on without me. They will eventually not even remember me clearly.

Yes, I will become nothing—in terms of this temporal world—when I die. And yet, formless, I will dance in the night sky.

XIX

On an ideal day in the future, I'd get up at 6:00 and spend the morning in a similar way as now—reading, meditating, reflecting and writing, doing yoga, watering plants, showering, and so on.

After lunch, I'd go out and run errands with Greg or with friends, or look at art or listen to music, or go for a walk or hike. Later, I'd have a nice, simple supper at home or in a quiet restaurant with Greg and perhaps with friends. Afterwards, we'd enjoy conversation, a card game, a video — or, if we hadn't walked earlier, we'd go for a walk now. We'd read and talk and then go to bed at 10:00 or 11:00 at the latest.

This is not very different from what I'm doing right now. I guess I'm already living my "ideal day."

XX

Saw B. today. Fascinating! She says I have lots of help from spirits but that I have to direct them. Tell them that what I really want them to do is to guide me— forcefully if necessary—on this inward journey of discovering who I really am and of hopefully healing my body from cancer.

* * *

I'm watching my mind and noting the thoughts. My belly is full; there is slight nausea. I will phone Dr. G. today about the scan and the possibility of radio-ablation. I wonder when the cancer metastasized to the liver. There's a lot of fear and also fatigue. I'll skip practice for now and sleep.

XXI

Since I am in perfect health, other than this cancer, I believe I could be one of the people who can make enough changes that I will no longer be a fertile ground for cancer to grow. I believe my cancer grew because of my fears and sadness and despair. I thought I had understood and let go of these feelings years ago, but I never had the tools then that I have now. Then my focus was on understanding where these feelings came from; but that wasn't enough. Now I am learning to give them to God.

Yes, I believe I am able and motivated to change myself and stop the growth of cancer in my body. I am asking God to guide and help me. And I have the support of my husband in doing this work, which makes a huge difference.

XXII

The Dancer is my image of my ideal physical self. The Dancer is graceful, sure, confident, always moving, and full of energy and vitality. She reminds me of me as a child: on the monkey bars; riding my bicycle down Park Avenue or through the orchards; hitting a baseball perfectly; learning how to ice-skate in my mind; climbing sure-footedly in the woods; running and doing the long jump; catching Dukey for his bridle. And the Dancer reminds me of me as an adult: dancing when I first came to Toronto; scuba-diving in B.C.; running down Windermere at night last week.

XXIII

This morning I had a dream that I couldn't see. I was blind in both eyes except for a bit of light coming into the inner corner of each eye. I was upset, but somehow I went back to sleep. When I woke up, I could see just fine. Was this just a dream? Or was it an encouraging message about my spiritual growth? That a little crack of light is penetrating my blindness?

XXIV

Today our trip up to Bloor Street took longer than I expected. I became impatient and resentful of Greg, even though his business was also my business. I was anxious to get home and carry out my own agenda. Certainly, I was not living in and enjoying the Now. I was caught up in battling the "hostile" world which was keeping me waiting and holding me hostage. I forgot that I could see things differently—peacefully. I hope I'll remember next time. My health depends on inner peace. This will happen when I remember who I am—my mind, which can see things peacefully—not my egoic body which never sees peace in anything.

XXV

Today was a very good day for me. My energy and my mood were great all day. In fact, today is the second day I've felt 11 out of 10—10 being how I felt before I had my cancer surgery over a year ago. Actually, I feel better than I have in years. I can feel the energy of the Dancer inside me since we merged 2-3 weeks ago.

XXVI

We walk regularly. It uses up my stress energy. And, as often, I give my fear-thoughts to God.

  I'm doing meditation, attending my groups, going to doctor appointments, reading reports, talking to others about our physical condition.

***

If I live, I plan to continue my healing work for the rest of my life; to meditate daily; to read spiritual texts every day; to develop awareness of my connection with God or a Higher Self; and to become more united inside (not having inner conflicts but inner peace).

* * *

The groups I've been attending make a huge difference to our quality of life. We learn how to control our fears and thoughts, our physical pain (to some extent), and to grow spiritually. Certainly, we are improving our relationships with others.

It makes sense that as we become more peaceful and happier, our immune systems will work better and possibly slow down the cancer or even destroy it completely. However, we will all die someday of some disease or condition as our bodies deteriorate. Therefore, we may die of cancer.

XXVII

Years ago, when I left my first marriage and was in despair, I heard a voice say, "What you will need, you now possess." I then began to trust my Higher Self.

   Here I am again—working my way through a tangle of negative beliefs about myself. Clearing away another obstacle to awareness and going through the clouds on to the sunlight.

   I am one in a crowd of seekers. We're all looking for release from suffering and for inner peace and happiness. We're all searching for "the secret."

Lynda Rose died later that year—still at home. When she definitely knew her end was near, she asked her palliative care physicians to help her with an assisted death. Given our laws then, they had to refuse. Lynda next chose to stop eating and drinking and went into a coma. She died peacefully soon afterwards. I have not met anyone as brave and gritty, or whom I admired and cherished more.

Living with Sorrow

Grief is not about forgetting;
it's about remembering with gratitude.
—Rachel Naomi Remen

It is uncanny
you were here
a moment ago
now there is silence
like a raindrop
you have left
mystery remains
as eternal as nature

I am
frozen, stuck, powerless,
abandoned, paralyzed, and—
above all—scared stiff.
Life has lost all meaning.
What I feared
finally happened:
you died.
As a child I lived
to keep my mother alive.
As your husband,
I did likewise.
This time I failed
and as an old man
I am now orphaned
and widowed.

She's
not
here
she's not
here
she's not here
not here
here

This morning I took the bread
out of the fridge
and into the bathroom,
and realized that my grief
is an open wound.

Some days
I wish I had a wailing wall
to which I'd bring my sorrows.

Mourning hurts
and it is not
until I can feel
its immense pain
that I can accept
you are gone

I mourn you

My spirit is
like a bird shot
in the wing.
It flutters
but cannot get
aloft,
drags
itself across the
stony ground
of my monkish
existence;
finally,
drained
it crouches,
waiting,
as unresolved
sorrows circle
it.

I wish

I could tell someone,
"I'm scared." And ask,
"What about you?"
or, "Did you flee, too?"

Suspended

Everyone
whom we had nurtured
left after you died
I was alone
and could not face
the collapse of the past
nor did I see
a path into the future

What contract?

I had assumed
that if I treated
others well, good things
would come back to me.
Today I heard the cosmos
laughing. There never was
such a deal—only
magical thinking.

A regret

After the palliative care physicians told you they could not accommodate your request for an assisted death I wish I'd held your hand more often and told you that I loved you, but I was afraid this would interfere with your determination to now starve yourself to death.

Lynda

You were a lonely and neglected child, a 16-year-old who escaped her parents' home by becoming pregnant. As a maltreated wife and then compensating mother, you also livcd with the scourges of skin, breast, and colon cancer for twenty-five years. Through it all, you developed a noble and awakened heart that was sensitive to the pain of all beings.

You were exceptional—forthright, gracious and virtuous, vastly curious, adventurous, and possessed of great integrity.

You and I were kindred spirits. We gave one another a love that was its own reward. We pointed the way to the sacred in each other. We nurtured others and through this giving away of ourselves, we became rich. I could not have asked for more of life, and I will be forever grateful for the gifts you gave me.

Fate was not kind to you. It was difficult to know this because you did not complain and you had resolved early in life never to do to others what had been done to you. Unfortunately, you were not heard when young and learned to hide your feelings. It upset me when you kept your sadness, your hurt, your fear, and your anger to yourself— and I could not reach you.

It is hard to accept that you, whom I loved and knew to be pure of heart, were trapped in an existential maze and became convinced in childhood that your life would be a series of losses. You were more complex than any of us knew.

"As a child I always believed there was a secret to being accepted and liked and loved and that I didn't know it. Without that secret I would fail and lose. As an adult, I know I am a good person—capable and kind and able to solve problems. But below my consciousness, there lurks this early strong belief that bad things happen to me. It's not fair, and it makes me feel sad and powerless and also guilty. I'm resigned to accepting these losses as they happen with good grace. Somehow, they are my lot in life. There is a secret to having happiness but I don't know it even though I have searched diligently."

These are words of great despair.

Almost every morning before sunrise as you lay dying, I stepped out onto our balcony and watched the dawn unfolding and thanked God for the beauties of his creation of which you were one. I am grateful to have known you, to have loved you, and to have been loved by you. You were a warrior and certainly the most courageous being I have ever known.

Sometimes grief is complicated

Today I heard
a cardinal sing
out of love of life.
Why do I hesitate
to do the obvious:
step over my own shadow
and end this stalemate
of stuckness
which makes my soul suffer?
The answer, dear reader,
is that I naively believed
I saved my mother
from committing suicide
when I was a child,
but, still childlike,
failed to prevent my wife
from dying of cancer
when I was an adult.

In truth, I lost them both
and with them
the purpose I believed
I had in life:
to look after another.
It is time to grow up
and let go of controlling.

My hibiscus

My hibiscus blooms when its needs are met,
and doesn't when life is barren.
For one day its flower dazzles me,
then folds its petals and drops
as a seedpod to seek rebirth.

Morning

I enter the sky
and become eternal.
Solitude is my friend,
and together we visit
depths of soul
hitherto unknown to me
yet strangely familiar.

What is faith

if not willingness
to say yes
as I leap
into the void.

The dark night
is a mystery
and that is its gift.

If we knew God
we would not be human.

Sometimes my faith
is a mere ember
and I feel forsaken.

In the face of my loss
and of my grief...
In the face of my feeling
that the world has become
meaningless, my task is
to love again—not only those
who are easy to love,
but to love myself.

Ghosts

The years from 1945-48 were very intense and entirely devoted to survival. I was needed and my mother depended on me.

It feels as though I have recreated those years in my relationships.

I also feel as though I was arrested in this time period. I have always remembered it as the most vivid time of my life.

It was a time when I was devoted to keeping my mother alive and when we had the closest connection we ever had.

By contrast, I had the same experience with Lynda—a close connection and desperately trying to keep her alive. But this time I felt I failed, and I think unconsciously became the orphan I had feared becoming in childhood— abandoned, alone, and bereft.

I believe it is these two hauntings I continued to experience as despair, hopelessness, a wish to die, and unwept tears. And it is here that I was stuck in unresolved grief—still wishing to change destiny.

When you died

I did, too, in the eyes
of your children.
If one doesn't know who one is,
if all of one's life
one has played a role--
then one has nowhere
to be at peace,
find a refuge,
be one's Self.

I am adrift

but near to home—
will this sorrow lessen
when the love of all
is restored to me?

Dear grandson,

you are often in my thoughts
and always in my heart.
I have wondered
how your soul has,
over the years,
dealt with the sorrow
over Lynda's death.
And I wish that your spirit
has found new hope
and meaning in life since.
I regret that you and I
were separated by the actions
of others who were stuck
in grievance and recrimination.
I want you to know
that I continue to love you
and care.
Blessings to you.

When you were dying you said

go
be as light
as a sun sail
and leave me soon
to love again

Lynda

This morning
as I entered the world
of meadow, trees, birds,
sheep, and wildflowers,
I felt you around me
and we became one again.

Thank you!

Thank you, too,
for your generous hope
as you lay dying
that I have another
good marriage.
I will live
as you wished me to
and not dwell on my losses,
but remember the gifts
we gave each other
with gratitude.

Remembering you

When you died, I blamed myself for not doing more, for not being more insistent in support, in love, in honesty. I had become your partner but not the confidant to your inner secrets. I did not know your strength hid your life-long expectation of doom.

When you died, my life stopped. I did what I had to do—obituary, funeral arrangements, eulogy, family get-together—and then I got sick. Heart problems. I spoke to the specialist of my broken heart, and he told me not to bother seeing him again. Your children and grandchildren pulled away, became distant, and I felt despairing and hopeless and stuck.

I entered groups, saw therapists. I spent days sitting in gardens we had loved and walked trails where we had been at one with all. I reflected on your life and ours to understand you and me better. Some peace, some healing began to happen.

I let go of my life-long wish to be dead.

Then something stared me in the face: I didn't know how to go on living without you, on my own—without crutches—something I had never done before. I had decided not to die, but now I needed to learn to live—standing on my own two feet. To give up being dependent, always helping but playing second fiddle. To live for myself and take care of myself, which is a novelty at the age of eighty-one.

Death, tell your tale to me! We fell short and didn't quite give each other what we needed. We failed ourselves. You are gone, and I cannot fix what was. Will I still avoid, deny? Or will I admit that life has changed forever? Will I leave the safety of my private world, and risk again in intimacy and in love? Will I allow myself to be vulnerable once more?

I still talk to you. Often, I apologize for failing you. Most of the time, I thank you. With you I felt deeply, found a family, became myself. Leisure has given me the luxury to enjoy what I value: the silence within; sunrise and sunset; birdsong; living in community; writing; painting; reading; classical music; quality conversation; organic food; walking and hiking; being kind to whoever needs it; supporting causes I believe in; and traveling occasionally.

Holding on to you was a source of solace. It allowed me to go on by myself. Now I can begin to let you go. I am no longer overwhelmed by the loss of you. I am safe to be defenseless again. The reality of your death is no longer shattering.

Mourning—though incredibly long—helped me to rebuild myself. Now I am not the man you married. I value solitude. I am stronger and more resourceful. I cultivate friendships and appreciate support. I am not as dependent as I was on you. I am moving forward still fearing sometimes to look back—when I must. Will sadness ever feel at home in me? There is no cure for grief. We knew that one day one of us would lose the other. Loss and grief come to each of us. But I will never forget you.

We bring our less-than-perfect selves to relationship. If we can bear it, we may allow ourselves to remember and face the real person we have lost—with all the impact she or he had on us—and face our fears and know our strengths. As well as theirs. However I choose to remember and understand our story will determine how I move forward. If I'm honest, I will recall you and me as we actually were. And then I will do better with others. I have held onto some furniture, pottery, sculptures, and books we collected to remember "us" by. I've also acquired a lot of new stuff as I'm building a new life for myself. We have a different connection today: you then; I now. I am grateful for what we had. So here I am, coming back into the world. You will always have a place in my heart as I move on. Given our love for each other, it could not be otherwise. But losing you has helped me realize that I can stand on my own two feet and take care of myself. It's a new reality, and I'm finally changing with it.

And I no longer feel that I'm betraying you by moving on and, perhaps one day, loving another again.

Stepping into larger shoes

For all that has been: Thanks!
For all that will be: Yes!
—*Dag Hammarskjöld*

After you died,

I became unmoored
and drifted. My life
had lost its meaning.
The love I felt for
you had been the star
by which I steered
my course. I see
that star still and it
insists I finish becoming
me—that I have come
too far to turn back.

Quest

In a dream I run a foster home for children under the age of six. We
are sent a boy in his late teens. He has suffered and been
transformed by it and turns out to be a surprisingly good fit in spite of
our initial doubts. After one or two years, he is ready to leave and go
out into the world. We are proud of him because to us he has the
potential to be one of humanity's champions. I am an old man now
and shuffle outside to the place of leave-taking. Before those
assembled, I say to him, "We have armoured you not with weapons
but with love. Go forth and be true to yourself with all."

Becoming

I chose to rebel
against my parents' clutching
neediness. When I escaped
home, the job of pleasing and
serving them went to my brother.
He had two choices:
submit or resist.
He gave them thirty years
and then died young.
When I was middle-aged, I again

had to look after my parents.
They hadn't changed,
but I had. Now I knew they had
sometimes done what they could
in spite of their own traumas and
deprivations, frequent poor choices,
and periodic rotten luck. Today
I thank them for what they did
give me: life and its basics,
and with it the chance
to struggle and grow to be the better
man I had not expected to become.

Glory be

I've reached a ripe old age!
I'm eighty-two and a day,
and I got here the hard way.
Sometimes I experienced goodness,
and it gave me hope.
Yet it was only when I underwent two losses—
the death of my wife and the end of my work—
that the cage door opened,
and I walked out into my own life.
To become deeper, to look after myself,
to be grateful for my gifts,
and to understand and accept my suffering.
Now I rejoice and actually want to live,
and do it gracefully and well.

The lesson

Having done my best to grow
and to encourage growth in others,
what other good choices
do I have in the end
but to forgive those

who were less conscious
and declined to accept responsibility
for their own lives
at the expense of others?

Forgiveness

You cannot forgive what you don't understand. Here is what I have learned about forgiving the harmful things ordinary, good people do.

What do I need to forgive?

My parents' acceptance of me was conditional.

From the age of six on, I was considered a "good" son when I was useful, made them proud, and served their needs.

The effect on me was disastrous.

I was unable to feel. I couldn't love or be loved. I believed that all human relations were transactions: I gave you something and got something back in return. I wished daily that I was dead. I tried to numb my pain and despair with alcohol and nicotine for thirty years. I was haunted by guilt that I had betrayed my parents and brother by distancing myself. And, until this year, I still believed that I was not worthy of love unless I earned it.

How have I learned to forgive?

I have struggled for years to forgive my mother, my two fathers, my brother, as well as myself.

All are now dead, except for me.

This is what I have learnt so far:

"Nothing human is alien to me," the Roman playwright Terence said. I realize we each do some good during our time on earth, and we are also transgressors against ourselves and others.

People often hurt others or are self-centered and dishonest as a result of their own unacknowledged pain, anger, and fears. My parents' upbringing was much harsher and less nurturing than mine.

Not everything started with me. I must be careful to face but not be burdened by the unresolved issues of my parents and grandparents.

It is essential to my own growth and healing that I forgive myself for my faults as well as forgive the trespasses of my family members. I have been as fallible as the people I blamed.

Forgiveness does not erase the past. A healed memory is not a deleted memory.

I heal through understanding and grieving and letting the anger and blame fade.

I realize that I protected myself from continued harm by leaving home when I was eighteen. I was also right to put boundaries on my dealings with my family from that point on.

Unfortunately, I took my woundedness with me.

As a result, I have sometimes hurt others which I regret.

I have tried to atone and forgive myself by rediscovering and reclaiming my goodness through therapy and being kind, honest with my feelings, and doing right by other people as well as myself.

In order to truly forgive, I need to understand what it is in me that made me vulnerable or susceptible to harm. For example, what blind spots do I have? What behaviours do I repeat that invite abuse—for example, my tendency to be a caretaker? What do I need to look at and deal with within myself?

In the process of doing that, I can let go of the outrage I harbour so that I can be free and not remain tied to the transgressor or their deeds. I have also come to realize the following:

Forgiveness is a decision and a process. It's not easy and it takes time.

Forgiveness by itself does not restore trust or relationship. But a reconciliation may happen, if I admit to doing wrong, make amends, and seek forgiveness.

Before I ask for forgiveness, I need to change the way I treat the person I have wronged.

Forgiveness and compassion are linked. I am accountable for my wrongdoing, and yet I deserve to be seen as human with a capacity to change.

Finally, genuine forgiveness does not deny my feelings about the hurt but faces them head on. I must grieve what happened to me before I can let go of my anger and resentment.

Paul Tillich observed, "Forgiveness is the highest form of forgetting because it is forgetting in spite of remembering."

I dreamed
I offered you my hand
to help you.
You took it
and did not let go.

Sunflower
you and I are
as we are
yet have one source
you are part of me
and I am part of you
I feel such joy

The soul

The soul seeks to be true to itself
and wishes us to become
who we really are.
This gives a life its worth
and its meaning—and makes
following one's calling to live large
in relationship, passion, service
a sacred, everyday task.

I walk in the woods

to the grove of red pines
and whisper my thanks to God.
Now I know why I am here—
to feel deeply and become
whole in this eternal now.

To whom it may concern

Thank you for allowing me to be here
and struggle.
I won't ask why or
bargain that my luck will hold or
wish that anything had been different.

I am just grateful that,
while I deal with new losses,
there is still purpose since you ask:
who am I, what do I want,
and where am I bound—and
as I answer, reveal a truer,
more meaningful me
than when I felt small and hid my shame.

My hour with God

Every morning
at dawn just before
the sun rises
I am given
a front-row seat
in the universe
and lean back
as the sky
explodes with light
and colour
it is then that
I give thanks
enter it all
and become timeless

Wonderment

I live
with an open heart
and experience everything
as though for the first time.
The beauty of creation
is embodied in any fragment
of its whole. Today
I looked at a leaf
and became the peephole
through which the universe
looks at itself.

Pale blue,

one morning glory
blooms today.
My heart rejoices,
and I realize
it is not conceited

to become oneself—
it is a duty.

Thank you

for humbling me
forcing me to grow up
and take responsibility
for my life
to grow and to change
so that my life
has meaning

The chain

The chain is now broken.
I stand on my own feet
and live thoughtfully, aware of my fears.
I have walked away from rescuing others.
My suffering made conscious
has released the ghosts of my past
from the sins they visited
upon their descendants.
Doing so I pray has healed
the sorrows of my dead.

Stillness

Snow falls.
The woodpecker at my feeder
sits tall—fast asleep.

Dawn unfolds
never the same
and always breathtaking.
Each morning,
I am awed
and humbled.
Thank you!
I am my own man.
I am free to be a seeker.
I am alive to the world.
And I care.
Thank you for these gifts.
I bless life.
I thank the dead
and I resolve
to be kind
and true
again this day.
What had hardened
has softened
and my soul is still.
I have come home
and forgive myself.
My heart is open, and I embrace
the mystery of my journey
into the depths of this larger life
and my soul's evolution
to be one with All.

3

Before it is too late

What is not remembered of the past
is doomed to be repeated.
—*George Santayana*

For noble ends

The film is grainy and short.
A young nun wearing
a thick maroon-coloured coat
and conical yellow cloth hat
douses herself with gasoline.
She shouts, "I want freedom for Tibet."
And lights herself with a match.
Flames shoot up and outline her figure.
Onlookers scream.
A laywoman steps forward
and offers a white khata scarf
out of respect to the body
that has toppled forward.

The past is not the past.

It is a ghost
haunting us in the present,
which asks for an expiation
of the shortcomings of our
mothers and fathers
as we search for lives
of meaning in time to come.
May I be heroic
and not ask of you
what is unfinished in me.

Iraq: 2003-2011

"I hope what the Americans did to us, happens to them."—Young, noncombatant Iraqi woman who had half her face blown off by an American grenade.

The Geneva Convention states: "Any person not belonging to the armed forces is considered a civilian.... In case of doubt, a property which is normally assigned to civilian use should be considered as civilian and must not be attacked.... The prohibition of attacks on civilian persons and civilian property includes all acts of violence, whether committed in offence or defense.... The prohibition includes attacks launched indiscriminately."

Tormented by vulnerability, the United States is trapped in an endless use of force. At home, the soldier who so carelessly threw that grenade into that woman's house is hailed a war hero.

How do we expiate?

Here in Canada and in Germany today,
are the memorial anniversaries,
the commemorations,
the restitution payments,
just dumb shows and indulgences
ritualistically performed
to sidestep heartfelt questioning
and admission of national shame?
Would it be more genuine and helpful,
for example, if people in both countries
bestowed the love, care, and money
they lavish on their house pets
on poor people everywhere in this world?
Would that make both of our countries
better places to live in? And us better humans?

Decay

Few of us see the big picture,
understand how it all hangs together.
Know:
People feel left out in their own countries
and are deeply unsatisfied, even angry
and blame the elites. Change is coming.
It was the collapse of the middle classes

that brought Hitler to power.
Demagoguery helped.
U.S.A. (and Canada) beware.
Opportunists are always with us,
and it's easy to become primitive.
When good people are threatened,
you cannot be sure how they will behave.
Denial, silence, refusal of guilt
usually follow.
What is our future?

Before it is too late

America get your house in order.
Rid yourself of your vengeful cults
and deadly weapons that make us all suffer.
Beware the malicious mythomaniac actors
who would be your rabble-rousing leaders.
Honor honesty or lose trust
it still exists and is worth pursuing.
Prevent the dictatorship that destroys truth
and replaces it with lies that cater
to false hopes and base instincts.
Remember you fought for freedom
against Nazi Germany and Imperial Japan.

Retreat

Why have I come?
I can't stand the silence,
getting up so early,
all of me aching as I sit,
missing chocolate and cookies.
And endlessly, facing myself.
I want to go home.
Then there is a moment of peace.
A cardinal sings in the silence.

I am here in the present,
at-one with all as it is.
I am awake. The bell rings.

Why did he go to Jerusalem?

Until this point
he had acted upon
the dangers that surrounded him.
He avoided the towns,
the Pharisees, the Romans.
He preached only among his own kind.
But then he did everything to stir
Pilate's and Caiaphas's ire.
He led his band of disciples
triumphantly into Jerusalem.
The next day he assaulted the Temple,
overturned the tables of the money changers,
and freed the sacrificial animals from their cages.
So they came for him in the night
and killed him as they had the messiahs before him.
He had said, "Do not think
that I have come to bring peace to the earth.
I have not come to bring peace but a sword,"
and did what he was created to do—
liberate the oppressed.
By the way, he was not white
and there is no definite proof he even existed.

My I-ness seems unique
until I realize I am
thinking the thoughts of others
around me and before me.

For as long as I remember
I have been
co-dependent and survivor.

The questions I now have
are: which of me
has been host
and which was parasite?
And: will I always
need to be one and the other
to exist?
Or: can I give up both
by becoming whole?
I walk into the future
carrying the burdens
of everyday life
but releasing the dead
of the debt they owe me.

The search within

I have been alone
seeking to be whole,
know the sacred deep in me.
Not as others believe—
but on my own path
and in my own place.
I am present,
walk to and through.
You, my soul, and I
now meet again.

The heart knows what reason denies:
that out of darkness comes light
and that love will conquer fear.
Today, I learned
that instead of reflexively thinking,
"How do I fix this?"
I can ask myself,
"How do I choose to respond?"
Next, I may declare war

on, "Peace at any price."
Be gentle,
don't beat yourself.
Be open
to learning the truth.
Accept help
and don't be alone.

Soul, help me to dream,
to journey into my inner self
and show me how to live
as the man I really am.

At the edge

Suffering is a great teacher.
I have learnt from it while
a child of war,
the son of a raped mother,
rejected in love,
lost in addiction,
a failure at work,
at the bedside of my dying wife,
abandoned by friends.
Crisis helped me grow
and pain transformed me.
But the daily news violates me
and I suffer as I witness
accidents, disasters, killings,
political correctness and cravenness.
What I want from life
is wisdom, compassion, humility,
and freedom from the bleakness
of the non-scenic route
through a meaningless life.

When I catch myself

feeling sorry for my lot,
I remember the old ones
in Yemen already dead
as their daughters bend over cots
waiting numbly for their children
to follow next. It's odd—
when we have someone to look after,
say our dog, we forget that others
need our help even more.
When we add more to enough,
are we happier?

Inside the rabbit hole

much harm has been done
by those who believe
they know more or better than others.
"Hitler couldn't have been all bad,"
you say, "for he was a vegetarian
who loved dogs."
And, "Trump is like us
because he eats cheeseburgers."
I realize your enemy is not my enemy.
Your truth is not mine.
Conversely, my enemy is not yours
nor is my truth your truth.

She was a seed that blew in

and took root in the soil
to become a weed—
a pest to some
but a bouquet to the children
when she flowered

now shadows haunt her
she is a mirror
an echo chamber
hoping to be seen and heard
but hidden to herself

a genial iceberg trapped
like the insects in the amber she wears
as she appraises others
her favoured expressions are a frown
and "But...."
I wonder who long ago
murdered her young dreams
and demanded she live
their unfulfilled dreams instead

"Be kind,"
Philo reminds me,
"for everyone you meet
has a really big problem
including you."

To do list

let us throb to the same rhythm
find words to name the sacred
unburden ourselves of secrets they call sins
empty our hearts of loneliness that is too great
be a puzzle to those who never take a stand
or risk and are forever nice
expose the insidiousness of technology
whose helpfulness undermines our humanity
avoid landing on Mars to become rootless
prevent us from becoming gods or thralls
freaks whom even outcasts shun

This is suicide

Why are conservatives, of all people,
going out of their way to destroy
public trust in the judicial system,
public servants, politicians, and journalists—
the underpinnings of democracy?
Why are they so suspicious
and no longer believe in the common good?
Now the bills are coming due
on what they failed to do about housing,
health care, long-term care, and the environment.
Legal weed only goes so far in helping us forget
what we once had.

How to survive in a post-carbon era

You need water, food, clothing, shelter, electricity,
sanitation, transportation, medical and emergency services.
Don't expect to find these in a city
after inexpensive oil runs out,
the economy collapses, and the grid fails.
Prepare beforehand and learn personal survival skills.
Make yourself useful and be with others who contribute.
Then choose one world over another.
Learn how to live on little.
Know that the time to dig a well is not when you're thirsty.

Cripplings and choices

When I was twenty-seven, I was offered a vice-presidency. Something inside me hesitated and said no. I was already imprisoned by drivenness and affluence and more would kill me. They fired me for not being a company man. I then knew being on top of the dunghill was not for me. But I was also lost, no longer living a fictional life. I felt like shit and thought I had failed. Until then I had only known how to hurt myself.

My life was empty of meaning—deformed. I was numbed to feeling deeply. I had been stuck—a hamster running in place, going nowhere. I was wasting my life and had never been myself. I longed for a moment of reality—to know myself. I wanted to wake but chose to sleep. Whom could I imitate? Who might inspire me? I was a self but false. I had longed for love and been childish in my need to achieve. I wanted to be safe. I lived in my body but was afraid to occupy it. In a sick society, I wore the mask of death. I had arrived where I needed to be to begin again.

Many things have happened to me since that, at the time, were not in my best interest. They changed my life and made me more aware. I don't know where I'll go next and whether it'll be "good" or "bad." I can be with that and not want to hide or run away. I trust that I'll be up for it.

In my life's journey I've followed my nose. And always life gave me what I needed and pointed me in a new direction.

Yet we are more interested in how we present ourselves than who we are. I remember feeling I didn't matter, so I made myself important by being an asshole. So, who am I really; what is the actual story? Are my slogans my blankies? Or am I open to more than one narrative, more than one way of viewing the world?

I still ask: Are progress, consumption, capitalism the only choices? Do we wait for it all to collapse before we decide? We have no roots, no connection to the past or our culture. If your life is trashy, you become like trash.

Over time, mine has become a life in progress. I am now retired and realize you can't understand old age until you get there. Today I live in community. I seek out friends who are authentic. I sit and am part of nature—out of time. I lead a contemplative life full of peace. Solitude fosters my spiritual development. When I believe I've found the truth, I keep searching. I've come to know there are new ways to love: the intimacy of listening, of letting our lives speak, of your heart touching mine with your care. After a lifetime of losses and gifts given, I am still awed to be human and grateful for it.

Like Hitler before him,

the danger is that we,
who are not "the base,"
ridicule Donald Trump
because we find it inconceivable
that he has no conscience
and is a monster and take
our freedom for granted.
Yet his wound is his history,
and he must hurt others
before they hurt him.

In 2025 a delusional and paranoid tyrant,
surrounded by lackeys and bootlickers,
may again control the American nuclear codes.
False alarms caused by computer glitches happen.
This time, get ready to be here one second
and vaporized the next. Like Hitler,
he will have no hesitation
in taking us all with him.
The doomsday clock reads
90 seconds to midnight.

Paths of Grief

Humans are more stupid than frogs who actually jump out of a pot of
warming water. Instead, we rationalize:
My life is here in this pot.
I don't see anyone else being concerned.
It'll get better, so I'll wait.
They'll fix it, so why change?
Jesus will save me.
It's all happened before...and humanity survived.
It's a lie and really not happening.
Why should I change when they're not?
To hell with them; I'll look after myself.
What I do won't make a difference to the big picture.
I'm too busy...

It's my business, not yours: so, leave me alone.
It's God's will.
It's too late.
I know it's true, but I'm still safe.
I'm O.K.; the worst is yet to come.
The planet will be fine—there'll just be a lot fewer of everything.

The fear

After his shiny blue Porsche Tay was stolen
from his Thornhill home, John—a Toronto dentist–
paid a civil engineer $ 21,000 to install pop-up bollards—
retractable metal posts—in his driveway.
He was offered a choice of designs, colours and finishes
to complement his driveway esthetics.
He chose the silver package which includes maintenance services
like inspections, lubrication and occasional repairs.
Does John now feel safer?
"The car can be replaced," he says.
"But what happens if someone breaks in
and I happen to stumble upon them?
Then we have a catastrophic situation."
Good point, since John's German shepherd, Rolf,
slept right through the car theft.

"It's a sad state," John says.
"It's every man for himself."
He is now in talks with a security company
that offers a form of artificial intelligence
to analyze and act upon video images
of any intruder approaching his vehicle or home
and will dispatch help.

Solitude

And the day came
when the risk to remain
closed tightly in the bud
became more painful
than the risk it took
to blossom.
—*Anonymous*

Solitude

Ultimately, each of us is alone,
and life is unfathomable.

You and I have known each other
since I was a child.
Even as I wasn't aware I had rights
to care, to understanding, to friendship,
you stood by me,
became my companion.
I was silent, but you knew
the desolation of being different,
not valued.
You became part of me—
I accepted you, lived with you,
and let you be.
Thank you for the pain.
Sometimes, you were a source of shame,
and I tried to escape you
only to discover terror.
Then, after dark nights of losing you,
my soul found you again
in a moment of communion.
Now you were wanted
and I felt a longing
that had no name.
You became a natural part of my life.
You felt like a long dark rainy day.
You were my teacher,
my introduction to integrity,
to wisdom, to my self—
to a new life.
You made me whole.
Through you I saw and knew
I was human.

Today, I value you as my comrade.
You are my quiet place.
With you I retreat from the world

content that I am the possessor of nothing,
not even that cloud in the sky.

A waif, she

Your beginnings were shaky.
Your darkness, helplessness,
born of having been a victim
long ago. In those looking on,
you aroused sympathy—
they wanted to take care of you.
To your children you said,
"Life is too hard."
And lived to prove it.

You left this life
empty-handed
not having found
one person who loved
you for yourself.

Now the essential questions are:

What am I learning about myself
as a result of your death?

And
How is your death transforming me?
Niceness is a tyranny
and a lie.
It is the brother and sister
of hypocrisy.
It knows what's best for you
and will try to control you.

Niceness shuts you up.

I regret standing by
silent, half-believing

you deserved to be judged
a nuisance.

Your face mirrored
your vulnerability,
your pain, your need
to be cared about.

Even though I let you down,
I thank you.
I will continue to learn from you
and what happened
for a long time.

Welcome

I give you salt and bread
and wish that you will find
in yourself and among us
everything you need.
We are no longer alone
to face the unknown
and sense there's meaning
to the lows and highs
we call a life.
What is sacred to you?

So

when did you become you—
aware of your self,
your inner world, and others?
When did you first feel love
and when did you assert being you?
Were your parents mature enough
to allow you to rebel,
to be different from them?
And are you now at peace

with yourself and then another?
I am charmed by your naturalness
and pray we will respect one another,
trust we can depend on each other,
and want the best to come out in the other.

Phoenix

that face is open
her direct gaze
unavoidably penetrating

false witnesses they
sit stunned
as they realize
she is true and real
and they are not

my naked soul
is deeply touched

Alone

Sometimes my soul grieves
and I am lost, lonely
and long to reconnect
with another, be it God
or an accepting presence.
It is then that I wish
I could tell someone
how much I miss
the connection I lost
when you died.
Yet I hesitate
to go through your papers...
It's like opening a vein,
and I dread the pain.

Asperger's?

I was a loner
which allowed me to avoid
taking the chance
I might be rejected.
Alone, however, I was lost.
I wish I had at least
been systematic.
Instead,
my life was chaotic
until one day in middle age
you loved me,
and I learned to love myself.
Though you died,
I am now at peace
but again, feel alone.

The heart knows what reason denies
that out of darkness comes light
and that our love will conquer our fear.

Connection means protection,
and so, it is easier to engage the unknown
holding the hand of another
than to do so alone—
even after the worst is over.

Now I walk a road I did not choose.
With you dead, I have no one
with whom to share
my fears and desolation.

Oddly,

I am not lonely
as I dance alone
to the rhythm
of my broken heart.
Since you died,
I have come to enjoy
solitude.
Though you may be gone,
we continue to meet
unexpectedly, out of time,
"How are you?
I still love you.
What's it like?"
tumble out.
We are enchanted again.

I feel

my irregular heart beat —
the rhythm of a broken heart
and hold the sorrows of all those
who have lost a love in this heart.
Be vast and then nothing.
Fear not the silence
or the darkness.
Instead, rest in that
which witnesses you
and be amazed.

We die so alone
waiting for another
to take the first step
of saying—something.
I am angry. I am sad.
I love you. Forgive me.
Thank you for everything.
But wait.... tell me about that
which we never spoke of—
the secret which,
unbeknownst to both of us,
created our fate.
Sixteen years ago
I climbed into the grave with you.
I am still searching for a reason
to shake the clay off my feet.

The dating site

How are you faring in this supermarket
of romantic illusions and delusions
in which you invest such undue hope,
casting your daily net of dated photos
and pastimes wished for but rarely pursued?
When will you realize that you burden
relationships with a freight of expectations
they cannot carry? Know that "love" is not
the only source of happiness and that as you age,
it becomes less important than finding the inner strength
and passions that make a life worthwhile.

Reverberation

Our gifts of grace,
the words of love we spoke
are now petals scattered
by the lily pond

where we once sat.
I close my eyes
and feel the joy
we shared.
I'm not sure
I have it in me
to do this again—
to love, to know
another, to create
a new life and home,
and then perhaps
let go once more
to be alone again.

Humans need each other

To feel alone
is to slowly die.
One is most one self
when connected to others
and least when detached from them.
Who would we be if we were
not loved when young
and accepted when grown up?
Could I accept myself
if you did not?
Would I know who I am
if you did not see me?
Is life for some just a doodle?

Four Seasons

One way to open your eyes
is to ask yourself, "What if
I had never seen this before?
What if I knew I would never
see it again?"
—Rachel Carson

Spring

It's spring,
and you're here to breed.
Yet the odds are against you,
and your numbers dwindle.
> * * *

Existence has no
beginnings or endings.
There is only change.
A rock becomes sand.
I am oft-born
and may be your distant
relation, small seed.
> * * *

A golden finch
visits my feeder alone.
"What's it like for you?"
I want to ask.
> * * *

I like to think
that the red-winged blackbird
which visits my feeder
in early May, pouches
the seeds it selects
so carefully to take them
back to its nesting mate
as a thanks for their shared destiny.
> * * *

Today,
I watched a robin
bathing and I, too,
felt cleansed.
> * * *

I feel sorrow
for the land that is being stripped
of its soil, for the trees once
full of starlings, for the hawks
that swept across this field,
for the millions of bustling creatures

living in and just above it, for the little
children who no longer race through it
and shout their joy, for the gardeners
who tended it in vain, and for the loss
of nurturance that this view
once gave my soul.

Summer

Despite abundance,
the birds at my feeder
take only what they need.
They are not their own
problem, as are we,
unless we recover our own life
and heal our wounded soul.
       ***
You must look
in order to see
and become enchanted
by a red pine,
a right whale,
or....
       ***
In Pella, the sunflowers
nod their heavy heads
eastward, awaiting
Alexander's return.
       ***
In nature
everyone
is watching
everyone else
as each manages
to coexist.
No one claims,
"My fur is lighter
than yours,
so I deserve

to go to the front
of the watering hole."
* * *

It is a mystery so vast it overwhelms me.
I find it in a baby's penetrating gaze,
touching the bark of an old-growth cedar,
the trust of a chickadee landing in my palm,
and the dazzling radiance of a slow sundown.
I am holy sometimes.
* * *

The grackles sit on bare branches
grumbling that the meek
and the relatively weak
always come first at my feeder.
The world has gone to hell
in a hand basket since I was a chick,
some screech like rusty hinges.
The bullies among them
especially look over their shoulders,
as they're frantically feeding
when I'm not there to stand watch.
* * *

The problem with my life is that
it only knows how to repeat itself.
Today, a Cooper's hawk sat six feet from me.
I was so shaken, my whole being surrendered.
Now my soul summons me
to have a conversation
about the meaning of my life.
I feel like running but know it is time
for my next lesson.

Fall

The fox trots by
so skinny I want to tell it
to slow down and save its energy.
* * *

Leaves are beginning to fall.

I sit beside a blue jay
that is dying in my feeder.
Its leg is injured; its eyes are glazed;
its beak hangs open in a voiceless cry.
It is utterly exhausted
as it faces the setting sun
while a breeze ruffles its feathers.
The other birds that usually feed here,
stop and pause and then pass on.
This is a peaceful place to abide
one's last moments.

It is a slow, long dying.
A healthy blue jay lands
beside thc wounded one, screeches
and jabs it with its beak—
a weak flutter.
Then slowly the brightness drains
out of the dying bird's plumage
as it hunkers back down again.
Its hunched body shudders and shrinks,
and the bird turns inward.

Finches and sparrows fly by
ceding their custom to this fading
no longer giant. Evening falls.
The bird and I sit alone.

Before I go to bed,
I check on the bird one more time.
It is gone, and I am awed
and hope for the best.

This morning I put out more seed.
No birds come.
Is suffering palpable?
Does it linger?
Who knows?
I hear a harsh, raucous cry,
and a blue jay lands in the feeder.

I went for a walk in the woods this evening.
On the edge of the ravine, in a circle,
lay the bright blue feathers of a jay.
No bones, no skull, no legs.
All taken by the hawk that circles overhead.
***
The hawk doesn't come here anymore
Nor does the fox.
Nor the hare.
Nor the coyote.
The trees have been cut and shredded.
The topsoil has been removed.
I'm looking at a dusty field,
and I'm sad and angry.

Soon we will have wealthy neighbours
living in monster houses
who will not know or care
what was sacrificed for them.

Winter

Like fireflies
filaments of snow
flash silvery
in the bright sun
as the blue jay
hacks fiercely at
frozen seeds that
fly in all directions
to the delight of famished
sparrows.
***
Like a blanket
the weeds on the berm
fold in on themselves,
are covered with snow,
and hug the earth
until next Spring

141

when the seeds I sowed
will emerge as wild flowers.
*　*　*
In deep winter
a hungry hare
crossed my path
and I thought,
"Dang! I should always
carry a carrot."
*　*　*
Usually, I'm a vegetarian
but then we ate the chicken
that ate the maggots
that were in the manure pile.
I'm trying to figurc out
what to say to this chicken
when we meet in Heaven.
I might say, "I wish
you'd known how to fly."
Or, "Death is an enigma
which completes the circle."
Or, "You tasted pretty good."

The natural history of capitalism

We are in the beginning of a mass extinction,
and all you can talk about is money
and fairy tales of eternal growth.
— *Greta Thunberg*

The natural history of capitalism

Until February 11, 1937,
GM workers in Flint, Michigan,
were forbidden to talk to one another
during lunch breaks.
They were routinely fired
when they turned forty.
Today these workers' grandchildren are underemployed,
and their children are dying from opioid overdoses.
Tomorrow they will support a war,
and GM will be humming again in the US of A.
The business of business is business.

The last four decades were years with few rules
when morality became an abstraction.
As rich white males raped the land,
the geography of the American mind changed.
Corruption, injustice, inequality, industrial collapse,
unemployment, deaths of despair, and climate disasters
bred anger, contempt, apathy, and cynicism.
Capitalism is running its course and no longer delivers.
It is replacing itself with global corporate monopolies
which defy governments, obliterate the common good
and devour its carcass. Have you noticed
that three men who own these corporations
have more wealth than the entire bottom half
of the American population, or 170 million people?
Or that ten per cent of our wealthiest citizens
are personally responsible for forty per cent
of our pollutants? Or that, beyond money
and power, these people are clueless.
Neoliberalism creates big winners and big losers.
You may not want to know this
and would rather live an untroubled life,
but extreme inequality rarely ends well
and often does so violently.
The powers of the self-perceived victims,

confused and unruly,
are to be feared for their fury.

Factory

abandoned machines
debris
fetid water
cracks
shards
rust
trash
dust
once
they made furniture
here
and this was
a place of pride

There are voices I trust.
They speak of the industrial age unwinding,
cheap energy disappearing,
pandemics sweeping the globe,
human numbers shrinking,
the climate shifting and causing
refugees to flow across borders,
political and military power unravelling,
travel becoming a luxury,
species ending up in trouble....
History keeps repeating itself, slowly,
as we revert to an era of scarcity and salvage.
A privileged elite
created the United States;
an angry mob will destroy it.
You have a dark soul, America.

In nature

everyone is watching
everyone else
for clues to survival,
and no one ever takes
more than they need.

Among humans
who don't consider themselves
a part of nature,
we get hyper-survivors
who put us all
at incredible risk
because they want it all
and are as gods.

Neoliberalism =

screwing someone else
to make yourself richer—
forgetting
that, in the end,
such a system
screws us all
and rots our souls.

Notes from la-la land

Nothing is ever lost but returns as fate.
Cut-throat neoliberalism and social media
stacked the deck.
They made us very sick.
And getting richer has not made us happier
though being poor still sucks.

Inside our own bubble, we are heedless.
We don't know the disease we are
as we infect each other with fake news,
false promises, and greed—
substitutes for real life.

Change accelerates;
impacts are greater;
collapses nearer at hand.

On the day the debt-fueled economy stops growing
and the endless boom bursts,
naked bankers and politicians
will blame you and me for hiding
behind blind hope and avoidance.

Someone asks: Will Jesus arrive in time?
Or the space brothers?
Others will tell you what you want to hear
for you have solar panels on your roof
and a veggie garden in the back.

Though we understand our worth as humans,
what can't go on, doesn't.

When big deadly came to visit

Nobody remembers the Spanish flu.
There are no monuments to it,
almost no mention of it in our history books.
It took its toll in thirteen weeks
in late 1918 and killed 50-100 million people,
perhaps more than the two world wars combined.

Women on all continents bore the brunt of it.
They nursed the ill.
They laid out the dead.
They took in the orphans.
They bridged the past and the future.

The infected smelled of musty straw.
Their hair and teeth fell out.
Many were delirious.
It all happened suddenly, silently.
One day you coughed, felt dizzy,

couldn't smell, felt weak,
took to your bed – then died.

The Americans blamed the Spanish.
In Brazil it was the German flu.
The Poles called it the Bolshevik disease.
The Persians blamed the British.
And in Africa, they called it the "white man's plague."

What invisible hand was at work here?
Why did it cut down fit men,
your neighbour but not you?
If this was the wrath of God,
what had that man done that you hadn't?

The disease was disgusting,
and threatening and to be avoided.
Still, one sneeze later, the flu was inside
your town, your home, you.
You isolated, you heeded the orders,
but eventually fatigue set in.
Why do this when others will not?

If you could pay, you tried your doctor.
If you had faith, you saw a healer.
Doctors offered you aspirin, quinine,
arsenic, alcohol, mercury, bleeding.
If you preferred home remedies,
there were mustard poultices, sugar lumps
soaked in kerosene, infusions of swamp root.
In India you saw a witch doctor.
In China you smoked opium.
Sometimes, the cure worked.
Other times, it made things worse.
You were more likely to die if you lived in India;
were a newly arrived immigrant in the U.S.;
ate a bad diet and lived in crowded conditions;
worked as a maid in Paris;
or as a gold miner in the Rand of South Africa;
participated in large gatherings;

already suffered from malaria or TB;
cared for the sick in your family;
had a genetic vulnerability to the flu.

One in three people on earth
had fallen ill with the Spanish flu.
At least one in ten of the stricken ones died.
My mother's mother was one of them.
My mother was inconsolable as she lay
crumpled and whimpering in front of her dying mother's door –
not allowed to see her. She spent the rest of her life
unsuccessfully trying to find another mother.
Children are usually burdened with the unlived lives
of their parents, and so was I.
I lived with and tried to ameliorate her sadness
and despair from my earliest years on.
It's a cross I still carry,
though now I do it consciously.
I wonder why Donald Trump, as he dealt with
the Covid-19 pandemic in the United States,
didn't mention that his paternal grandfather
died of the Spanish flu. Especially since
the insurance money for that death seeded
the family's real estate fortune.

The Roaring Twenties were fueled by euphoria at having escaped
the horrors of the First World War, the Spanish flu,
and the assorted upheavals that accompanied them
as well as by the deep-down fear and foreknowledge
that such cataclysmic events would happen again.
In the meantime, silence helped the world forget.

Whatever is

is
but I don't have to put up
with evil
whereas if it is good
I sing praises
we who live in silence
wait for the revolution
which always comes

In difficult times

too much happens too fast.
Our heads spin,
while some tell stories
about secret causes,
our troubles are obvious.
The evil sorcery that is AI,
the disaster of climate change,
the conflict between open
and closed societies
spell destruction for humankind.
Never say magic words
to a broom because
some gifts don't stop giving.
Yes, biology matters,
divides, and leads to discrimination.
But we don't talk about the cataclysm
caused by our workers losing
their full-time jobs and decent wages—
that they are now exploited,
impoverished, demoralized,
and turned off by those in charge.
It is now likely that AI will overtake
human intelligence in all possible tasks by 2050.
There is no alternative, we're told
by the ones who prosper from this tragedy.
The endgame is near—
religion and blaming are

making a come-back
as darkness looms
and intolerance and persecution
become the fashion.
Then the disgruntled shall inherit
the earth—such as it will be—
form an alliance
with an orange king
and fall upon the privileged class.
Who will become the monastics
of our dark age?

This is Canada...

We treat our lawns and pets
better than our old people,
the homeless, or the animals we eat.
And yet we insist
on happiness for ourselves.

How many forget their own suffering,
their professed faith,
when they begrudge the beggar
his crust of bread and would
kick it out of his hand
were that not unlawful.

The truth is not difficult.
It is in fact simple.
Humans need the security
of supportive structures.
We are not meant to be small, alone,
or sufficient onto ourselves.
And, if that is what we become,
we do not endure. Humans deserve
worthy work and not to be
slaves to machines. We deserve
lives of dignity, purpose, and meaning.
Without these, we die deaths of despair.

And with us, so will those
who brought this on.

Even as the inferno rages
and life feels shattered and broken,
I sometimes feel the sacred in all
and myself part of a holy web,
comforted by a song of protective love.

You name the problem

This is a snake pit,
and the mandated attitude is apathy
as well as self-satisfaction.
Even if the ship is sinking,
you pretend not to notice
and keep your mouth shut.
Still, it's hilarious
that we're mass-producing
electric vehicles which require
huge quantities of metals
and petroleum-derived materials,
the concrete roads we drive on.
The sun will never set;
the day will never end.

We've been taught
that we can always have
what we want,
and that there's a solution
for every problem.
But Reality sucks.
It ain't so.
And so, we throw tantrums.
Or someone else
throws them for us,
publicly, in prime time.

The evil we are

We're in deep trouble
and we don't care
about anyone else
except ourselves
when it comes to
our democracy,
our climate,
our environment,
even our own.
Slowly we slide
over the edge
into the abyss—
silent and pretending
to be asleep.

Even though
we are in a long descent
and even though
the Chinese may eventually
oppress us, I am on the side
of my plants—growing
inexorably towards the sun
standing tall
till the end of our season.

And if I were a perennial....

Too late

Ever wonder what it's like to be a duck,
not knowing what came before
or what is yet to be—
but only what is now in this little pond?
I was a fool to listen
to the malignant normality preached
from pulpits, lecterns, and parliamentary benches.

Our problems are of our own making.
We are past the tipping point
and are daily making the planet less livable.
All we can do now is try to slow the pace.
We are dying a needless, pointless death.
I used to think the meaning of life
is to know we are a small, beautiful note
in a larger concordant composition
that is our world. We mattered
and would be remembered for it.

Waiting for a miracle

Climate change is a problem
with no acceptable solutions
except delusions and placebos.
Self-interest reigns over
reality and principles,
future generations of humans,
and other life on earth.
We all want to continue
living as we do now.
After you, Alphonse....

Now a new colonialism is afoot.
Wealthy predatory nations like China
are acquiring agricultural land
in troubled countries.
There they grow food exclusively
for themselves using their own farmworkers.
You can say it's the market at work;
in truth, it's a scramble to snatch food
out of the mouths of the poorest of the poor
in Ethiopia, Mali, the Congo, and Sudan.
And I keep sending money
to the World Food Programme.
Am I pissing into the wind?

Autopilot

What was the computer
of that self-driving car
"thinking" when it struck
and killed a woman walking
her bicycle across the street?
The auto company said,
it had too many robots
working its assembly line.
"Humans are underrated,"
it told the *Wall Street Journal.*

He chooses not to choose

and will not read the paper
or watch the evening news.
"A pox on all your houses,"
he sometimes says and hopes
this detachment will keep him safe

even as his neighbours elect
a demagogue to be their
and also his next leader.

You can stick your head in the sand,
you can say it's not my business,
but one day you'll be next,
either to do their bidding
or to be their victim.

Senseless and sad

Our lives are coming apart at the seams.
There is a great divide
between those who have
and those who feel left out.
Memory has been lost;

there is no vision or gratitude.
We destroy and consume
and are joyless
while a great tragedy unfolds.
As climate change becomes disaster,
will we the people
rise up and demand change
as we have done before
when pushed to the limit?

Who are we?

CBC called the Israeli attack
that freed four hostages
and also killed 210 Palestinians—
mostly women and children—
as well as wounded 400 more
a success.
Does one Israeli life equal
fifty Palestinian ones?
And what does that imply?

I believe the next major war
will begin in the Middle East.
Evil will be pitted against evil.
Evil will win as well as lose.
We are the species that never learns
from the lessons of its own history.

2040

The world is finite
and we have overshot
its limits. Still, most of us
believe that technological magic
will save us from collapse.

As we play chicken with the earth,
someone should remind us
that nature does not blink.

Will you and I then decide to abandon
undue consumption and competition,
and only believing what we can see?

More likely, a self-programming robot
with artificial consciousness
will one day look us in the eye
and command us, as though we were dogs:
"Clean up your mess!"

The shape of unspoken things

By 2065 progress will make us gods
and everything will seem possible forever
unless a supercomputer or nature turn on us,
and "they" will have to come up
with something superior.
I suspect we will in the end
worship the wonderworking jaw bone
of a child man who had orange hair.

We took the course of least resistance
and gave up the vision
of a better tomorrow for our grandchildren.
Now we are uncomfortably silent
knowing the way we live has no future.
It's late, but we can still use less
in our own lives.
Even if one day sheep will graze
in the Rogers Centre,
I can't use less
because I don't want to be
mistaken for someone poor.
My creed is progress
and even as I betray myself

and the weak in our midst,
the end of this world
is the beginning of a next.
Don't blame me for the changes
you are not making.

There is one minor detail:
if God exists,
what's his take on this?
He created us.
So, who's responsible for the mess?
Or, is faith absurd?
And God only reputed?
Who is in charge?
Us, when we feel
like doing the right thing?
Not us, when we don't?
We replaced you, God—
whether you existed or not—
because you got in the way of progress.
You became an inconvenience.
And we, it turned out,
were not omnipotent and, therefore,
unfit to supplant you.
This is what collapse looks like.
If you listen, you will hear
the noise of the gravediggers.

Oceans will rise and swallow cities.

The land will become so hot
that food cannot grow.
Water will be scarce.
People will die and few babies born.
The fit and tough will join armed gangs
and become marauders
and do what bandits do.
Yet, while we have doomed ourselves,
to enter a dark age

we must continue to be kind to one another.
For compassion is our true nature.
I honour you for I see that which is holy in you.
And so, I find it in me.

Should you look a gift horse in the mouth?

The result of our profligacy
will be a new earth.
Those who survive
may curse our stingy legacy
but will continue to subsist
on the bountiful garbage
we leave behind.

The secret knows you

Humans, branded by the horror
of destroying other life on earth,
cannot comprehend their own death
and fail to recognize themselves
in the corpse of another.
I do not see beyond the shadows
amidst which I walk—
there is no world without me.

Ode to an algorithm

I remember the time
light revealed what was hidden in the shadows

and the goal of life was to find meaning in it.
Do you remember when we worshipped ourselves

on Facebook, and excess became normal?
Do you remember the day humanism died?

The day the bastards hacked our souls,
and the ultimate deception occurred

when we believed the bullshit story
we'd created to glorify ourselves?

The day we forgot who we were
and no longer resisted?

I have become a tame human
serving the digital dictatorship

of the ultrarich with the data
my body and brain generate in life.

2100

Down below,
skyscrapers jut out of the water.
This was once Miami.

In Lahore, Pakistan, the daily temperature
often reaches 60 degrees Celsius now.

4

God is a metaphor

Old age is very different from all the others
by virtue of being the last: it is the only stage
that cannot be outlived, and it is the final opportunity
to give definition to one's life,
the last chance to do and be what one values.
— *Stanley Jacobson*

God is a metaphor

that insists I act in good faith
and out of love; serve justice,
mercy and peace; give in a way
that is real and eternal;
sing my own song;
bind myself to another, and life;
come fully alive;
and set myself free—
to know who I am,
even though the person
I could have been never lived.

On turning eighty-five

I'm sure they were
drunk
when they burnt
every photo of me
in the Franklin stove
that night.
I'm sure, too, that
as they murdered me
my soul blazed bright
in the dancing flames.
For I am alive
and sane and sober
today
and more grateful
than ever.

Once

Once I had a family.
Then my wife died.
She had held it all together.
For a while I tried to walk in her shoes.

I gave what I could.
Her daughters became independent.
Then they disappeared.
I am old now.
I still struggle with the need to be needed.

My self

At night, in a dream,
I'm at a train station
lost and confused amid the hurryings.
"Walk instead," an inner voice urges.
I do and am surer.
Now I ask questions—
like who and why and what and how—
to find my destination.
And if I fail,
I know I can just stand still and wait.
What I seek will find me.

Before the fall

Religion should come with a warning:
don't put all of your eggs into my basket.
Religion creates dependency
and encourages people to suspend
the kind of thinking that allows them
to stand on their own two feet.
I prefer us to venerate
that which is larger than ourselves—
be it a tree, an ancestor, a god, the sky—
without being grasped by its prophets.
Instead, alone, become absorbed in the sacred
as we join to assist others
and find the peace we are seeking.

Death, I must befriend you

yet keep some distance between us
as I still search for the sacred
and find it in the stranger, in me;
in joy, love, forgiveness; even in
acceptance of illness and you, death—
all that gives purpose to my brief stay
here on earth.

Returning

This is the time of wolves,
but someone somewhere laughs
out of love of life.
The ragged, starving, shivering horde
lift their heads in wonderment.
They have all known
the nearness of death.

As a boy,

you spent a summer
on your knees forced to cut the grass
behind your father's house with a straight razor.
In life, you were haunted by the memory
of a street vendor chopping the feet off a pigeon
and releasing it to flutter to death.
As a man, you cared, did your duty, but did not love
as you were loved.
Of all else, you had more than you needed
yet it brought you no content.
The question carved into the green marble
of your tomb slab is: *How to live?*
I wonder: Why did you—who had it all—
emphasize the pain of your life
in telling us your story? And why
did you not make more gold out of lead?

In the lottery of life

we have little control.
Chance and luck
shape most of it:
your parents, your country,
your status, your partner,
your health. But...
you must have hope,
give things a fair shot,
and enjoy life.
If you're in the First World,
share your good fortune.

A bubble

for a moment
glistens
then passes away.
So, I have flashes
of joy, fear, loss, love.
Always a story is told,
sky-like and ephemeral.

That which I leap into
when I die is alive
and embraces me
with bird song.

Still, I fear that heaven
may be silent when my time comes—
for sometimes in my life,
I was as supremely
self-centered as a caterpillar.

We had it all

I am grateful for everything life has given me—
particularly the chance to grow and change.
I lived through the most prosperous time in history
in a civilization now in decline as a result
of having been stunningly selfish, wasteful, and clueless.
I thought it was evil but could not separate from it.
Sadly, most of us never understood
that we are part of the world in which we live.
And so we destabilized the earth.

In the fading light

These falling shadows in our midst
will be us next. I prepare and,
after a lifetime of losses and gifts given,
I now partake of the ageless pleasure
of reading and am never alone
but live for a time in that wider world
of writers—kindred souls
whom I shall never meet
whose books keep me alive.
Solitude fosters spiritual development;
there is a time to speak
and a time to keep silent.

What will go on after me is a soft breeze
gentling you as you sit by the pond
reflecting that the meaning of life
is to know we are a small, beautiful note
in a larger concordant composition
that is our world. We matter
and will be remembered for it.
I have never been a shriver.

Reflections

1

I don't want to die in a hospital
where death is the enemy
and I have to hide my despair
to spare others and conform.
Instead, I want to be in a quiet,
sacred, and comfortable place
where I still matter
and my last conscious moments
add to the meaning of my life
and allow me to leave feeling
that being here had been satisfying.

2

I am a kind and generous person
who at times in my early life
was fearful, selfish, and immature.
I regret the hurt that caused.
It has been a privilege
to live a contemplative life
surrounded by good books
some of whose authors feel like friends.
In my life, I was meant to learn,
to grow, to heal myself and others.
I am grateful to have had this opportunity.

3

What will be my legacy?
I have listened as people
sorted out their problems and conflicts
and emotionally supported them.
I gave my grandson change to give
to street people which he still remembers.
I have assisted many to go to school.

I once helped a homeless man
survive winter under a bridge
and find housing in the spring.
I next encouraged an overwhelmed
and abandoned boy to persist
until one day he 'phoned to say
he now loved his life.
I have been an example
in how to be an adult to others
and, hopefully, freed them
to become true to themselves.

4

Rumi once said, "Do not be lonely.
The entire universe is inside you."

Becoming my next self

So here I am
quite suddenly grown old—
stooped, breathless, and stiff.
I look at myself in new photos
and am taken aback
at the sight of this elderly me
who is still agile of mind.
My friends have become venerable;
light shines through their skin
and in this silence we learn
to love being alone together.

To be inside myself,
become spirit pure and simple
and take a solitary walk
around the pathways of my heart
is my need. Time is no more
and I disappear into revering
a single yellow tulip.
Peace and contentment are mine.

I sense the divine and feel secure.
I don't have to understand anything
but merely be part of all.

Being old does not always make me wiser.
I hurt someone today,
in fact betrayed them—
not intentionally but carelessly.
And I feel terrible to have caused
another being such suffering.
My sorrow was met with silent anger.
I am sacred and I am profane,
not abstractly but naturally in everyday life.
How can I be so far sometimes
from doing what is right?

The interior landscape of my later life
is where my soul sings a song
that only the silent hear.
Sit still with me
and daydream of a realm beyond being
where we enter the source, become Atman.

The gift

It is so obvious:
old age is as special a time
of life as childhood was.
And as magical—
watching a leaf form,
hearing a cardinal sing,
tasting grapefruit juice—
all as if for the first time.
And so, with comforts:
fresh sheets, a scented bath,
sunshine on your face,
orange marmalade—
then all is well.

Journey

The Awakened One is inside us,
I am she, and he is me
buffeting and shaping one another
as the ocean does sea glass.

Likewise, the teachings have been tumbled
and transformed to deliver
the living truth that although—
all get old, sick, and die—
we can transcend our suffering
and become enlightened.
Stay awake, be decent,
and leave your rafts behind
we are told.

This is a subjective path
for one's whole, liberated life
where what we do
with what we are given
is what can make us free
and give us joy.
Be birthless and deathless
and always rebecoming.
With your heart filled with kindness,
compassion, joy, and equanimity—
be still, love all beings,
and cherish the mystery of existence.
Practise the virtue that is giving
with no thanks in return.

I reflect on the face of the Buddha
and find deep wisdom and compassion in it.
Looking inward, I glimpse these
in my and your own being.
Although prayer may not work,
it's good to do it anyway.

Entering old, old age

Once I was blessed with abundance
and lived like a gambler
on a winning streak.
It was a time of dreams
that lasted forever.

Today I search within
for a reason to be—
always aware of you
who is no longer here.
Starved, I hunger
for meaningful connection
yet hesitate to love another
again, in the face of their
or my certain passing.
For one thing is certain:
to be well is not to be spared.
Also, I value solitude,
the luxury of a contemplative life.
Old age becomes the place of separation
and, in the end, one is alone.
Where I live now is sometimes my home.
My neighbours whisper their stories to me,
ensuring we're not too close
but also not strangers.
Even when life feels dismal,
I am grateful to be here
not living on my own.

Why me?

I believe some cancers and other
illnesses happen
when our psyche receives a huge blow,
such as a perceived betrayal.
If it is the latest such experience of many--
going back into our past--
we feel abandoned and hopeless
and crushed in spite of our best efforts.
Perhaps out of shame,
we are unable to share this pain,
and see no reason to keep going.
Our spirit and then our body give up.
Any great loss, if ungrieved with others,
may do this.

Preparing for surgery

There is the joy of being alive,
of sunshine entering my heart
and feeling great gratitude
that I am still part of this
beautiful, beckoning world
which surrounds me silently.
The human spirit overcomes so much.
Thank you. I am at peace.

After the surgery

The smell was the worst of it:
unusual, metallic, morgue-like,
or perhaps more akin to that of a slaughterhouse.
A stench really of an inside dying,
a bleeding to death. How does another—
with few sick benefits—
tied to a machine in a factory,

enslaved at Amazon, or flipping hamburgers
and riding public transportation for hours
with no public washrooms around
manage this fear, this discomfort,
the constant urge to pee blood?

I trip over mystery

like the dead cardinal
curled up under my feeder
which trusted to the end
that this was a safe place.
Is the moment
when I slide from consciousness
into sleep like the moment
when I slip from life into death?

Prayer

In each of us
human consciousness continues to evolve.
Each of us is the blueprint,
the epitome, the cathedral
in which humanity celebrates its grandeur
and mourns the betrayal of its potential.

I call myself "I"
because I am conscious of being an island,
separate from others —
not knowing that the real "I" is vast
and mostly unknown to me like the universe,
without an understood beginning or a clear end.

I cut myself off from what were once my roots.
I was on the earth but not a part of it.
I lost my inner life, my soul--
they became hidden and I was lost.

You, who are sacred,
forgive that I doubted
and then denied you.
Money, power, another warm body,
accomplishments could not replace you.
At long last, you restored meaning to my life
and made me whole again.

I pray that I may be helped
to continue to heal and once more
live a life of the spirit.
At age eighty-six, may I become
what I was born to be.
Help me to understand
those who are unlike me
and offer them kindness.
Thank you for leading me here.

Many a morning in spring

when I awake
I remember 1945
and face nothingness.
I have no reason to live--
No dog, no child, no sweetheart
to greet, to continue
a connection that is easy
and everlasting in my heart.
Do I let go and drown,
or do I make another effort
is a daily question.
Once again I decide to live,
if only to have my morning cup
of coffee and watch the willow sway
and write these words
to whom it may concern
somewhere in that dark wood
I traverse more consciously.

Apparition

Every evening as I read,
one moth emerges from the birdseed I buy.
Attracted by the light of my lamp,
and the warmth of my body,
it circles me again and again.
It is like a spirit
seeking contact, connection, communication--
and is my only visitor.
Eventually, this becomes too insistent,
overwhelming, even frightening.
As it again buzzes my face,
I clap my hands loudly and kill it.
Is this murder or madness
or, simply, mere malcontentedness?

In review

Suffering, losses and old age
have brought me here.
War, chaos, emigration
as well as slow insight and learning
have framed my reality.
Sadly, I have not lived my own life
but acted from a script written by others.
Even when they were going well,
things seemed not quite right
because there was no "me"
with whom you could have
a deep, lasting, trusting connection.
To hide was the safe thing to do.
Only when pushed, did I rock the boat.
The turning point came when my wife died
and I retired. I chose to live, not die.
My soul found me and became my companion.
I wish I hadn't been such a slow-poke learner.
For all this, I blame no one—not even me.

It was

a colourful spring
and I was there,
a curious bystander
full of selfish expectations.
Life spoke to me
and asked me to listen
and to follow its call
to enter the unknown.

Time slowed as I stopped
giving my life away—
when seared by loss,
I found order in chaos.
Before the question had been,
"What does it mean to be—
to say you are?
To make yourself up along the way?"
There are real limitations in this world.
One is the paralysis of freedom.

I never had what is called faith
in the end as a beginning.
As I enter the mystery of death,
I count the success of my life
by the lives I have touched for the better.

Six Sermons

Sermon *n. lecture, homily, preachment, exhortation, moralizing, preaching, diatribe, declamation, admonition, discourse, lesson, disquisition, address, instruction.*

Climate change

I

Life is a gift,
and a forest
is a commonwealth
shared by all—
sacred
just by being.
It allows us
to know and feel
the truth that was
in a time of myths.

Every day I palm the same oak tree,
close my eyes until time is no more—
only this blessed moment.

Behold a russet leaf
and fall silent.
This is the way.

When we clearcut a forest,
it becomes a wasteland—
an altar to pain and grief
and to a nearly dead deity
from which the birds, the insects,
and the animals have fled.

II

Once, the sacred was not far-off, unearthly, distant.
It was a force, a presence found within,
in rite and in reverie.
It was the mystery that could not be explained.
It was the force that permeated all things.
It was the utmost truth.

It transcended all and consecrated nature.
Why then did we sever this link?
Was it to turn nature into an object
to be exploited?
God is now dispensable and humans
the masters of an Earth no longer sacred.

III

Until now, humanity has rarely faced
a problem it could not reverse.
Still, every age contains the seed
of its own destruction.
Ours is peak oil.
The great grief of our time
is the emergency brought on by too many
of us piddling in the pool we swim in.
85 per cent of the carbon that's been emitted
into the atmosphere in all of history
was poured into it during the last 30 years.
That's you and me!

The world speeds by.
Climate change happens inexorably
and mostly out of sight.
Not to act in the face of evil
is also evil.
God may be annoyed, but we act
as though we know his will.
In the dining room, she still believes
in progress, while he says it's all happened
before and will right itself again.
Isn't this February weather glorious?
"I don't mind climate change.
It's kind of nice," she says.
I face south, and the temperature in my place
is 29-30 degrees Celsius every day the sun shines.
And this is winter.

IV

Every night, 800 million people
go to sleep hungry—
while Canadians throw away
a fifth of their food uneaten
and whine about the cost of living.
A current forecast states that by 2050,
when an increased global population
and growing demand will require
50 per cent as much food again
as today, agricultural yields
may be down by almost one-third.

V

My generation lived hedonistically
and devastated the planet.
It still only wants to hear the good news.
We are dumber than frogs
who always jump out of the pot
before the water boils.
During this century, we will blow past
a global average temperature increase of two degrees Celsius.
The world's industrial economy will then collapse.
When we hit bottom,
food, water, land, shelter, friends, and mutual support
will be the things that matter
though greed will never die.

VI

The good news for the long run
is that our numbers are shrinking,
and we are slowly headed
toward a population bust.
Will fewer people also lower
the average global temperature

in time to allow the human race
to survive?

VII

Today is a beautiful day,
and it's hard to remember
that we just lived through
once-in-a-lifetime pandemics,
wild fires, storms, floods, and droughts.
Or to acknowledge that a couple hundred species
are going extinct every day,
and that the world as we know it
will soon end.

VIII

The junco and I sit facing each other.
The bird completes the landscape for me,
and I am its scenery.
Is it progress to steal from the future?

In the face of disaster, we retreat into distraction

I

Excessive technology gives us the illusion of mastery.
Those who have lost their souls
are now searching for them online.

We are lazy of heart and imagination.
We play at happiness, and our hope is blind.
We are antlike, digitalized and addicted,
as we worship the god who does our bidding
and gives us nice things which we deserve.

Yesterday's truth has become today's prison.
If there is a netherworld, is this payback
by all the former slaves and those otherwise oppressed,
or is this simply the result of stupidity, inertia, and greed
of the many encouraged by a few since World War Two?

II

Academia went silent long ago.
The media censor themselves.
Politicians become liars.
In my dining room, honest self-expression
is viewed as akin to farting in public.
We are all positive and polite.
To what end are we
desensitized and bright-sided?

We are all guilty,
since we watch evil done
and acquiesce by our silence.
Bystanders are complicit.

III

Self-censorship is rampant.
Disaster is normalized
and becomes entertainment.
Lies become the truth,
and what is destructive
is labelled benign.
The last sane voice is silenced.
Reality is lost; everyone becomes stupid;
and a demagogue speaks for all
in honour of falsehood, deceit,
distrust, and meanness.
Trump is our Nero.
"It's all a question of mind over matter,"
 a ruined soul says,
"We don't mind, and you don't matter."

Sometimes, a deep loneliness creeps into my heart

and I am bereft.
Then God stares back at me with empty eyes.
Would you be a Christ, a Bruno, a King, a Mandela, a Navalny?
If not, perhaps you haven't earned the right to know
you are alone in an indifferent universe.
Some made people feel and think and died for it.
Others returned knowing they would be killed.
Most of us saw only the pain and not the struggle.
As we live on in the hearts of those who knew us,
a few grapple with the complexity of heroes
and create the fleeting legacy we did not.

What started it?
Is there something that existed before infinity,
which created the universe,
which has grown as it has?
It is encouraging to think
that on a limitless number of Earths,
others are getting it right—for a change.

America has not changed.
The racism of Selma
has become the intolerant anger
of the Trumpists.
Bringing about social change
is like poking a hornets' nest—
there will be collateral damage.

At the end of our time,
let us comfort the afflicted,
afflict the comfortable,
let our hearts break slowly,
and exit with grace.
I am Cassandra, the dripping tap,
that gets on your nerves
with its insistence that greed is not good.
It is time to turn the lights out
and deny the wise ape
dominion over nature.

War is a business,

and there are no good wars
even if Americans have a president
who tinkles ice water.

War imprints you with trauma
for the rest of your life.
Only you know the fear, the evil,
the grotesqueness of the wounds,
the unreality and obscenity of it all.
You are changed forever.

Local imaginings state
war makes good people better
and bad people worse.
Women and children are always
its real victims. Is
homo sapiens a wise human?
Does a wise human value life
during their brief moment here?

Israel hold your own feet to the fire.
How can you lament the Holocaust
and not be angry at the genocide
of the American native peoples,
or slavery and Jim Crow,
or the destruction of the Palestinian people?
Those striped concentration camp uniforms
were modelled on those of the American chain gangs.
Does anomie encourage mass murder?

Dark brother,
even though you are gone,
you endure as a jointed soul
bonded with me in a common song,
and I ain't done sorrowing.

There was peace,

but in the summer of 1945
four times as many Berliners died
from starvation, disease, and suicide
than during the Allied air raids.

The city was eerily quiet—
an unnerving, silent skeleton.

Some say the corpses
in the concentration camps
were fakes. Elsewhere,
others realize there is no God
and weep.
In the meadow of death,
the dead speak their own magical words.
Cast out one of your own, they say,
and they will throw their shadow
over your children for three generations to come.
All secrets remain part of your story,
no matter your silence.
Suffering lives on.

A strong feeling of being overwhelmed
comes to me—as though things are too much
and I'm not up to it. This may be how I actually felt
at times in childhood but could not allow myself
to really know it.
As long as I am alive, I am not dead.
For I feel for me, see for me, remember.

I do not want to die
not having mattered to anyone—
without a trace.

You cannot be chosen to live

and not know suffering, sorrow or loss.
Yet a day will come when we dance
out of joy in the streets.
What is beyond and holy
becomes us and we know God again.
On that day, hearts break open
and we weep for what we squandered.
We awaken by seeing ourselves in another.
Each chooses their story
and lives it with hope, honesty and courage.
Small kind deeds often repeated
will change the world
and demonstrate our love for it.
We stand up for the weak and voiceless,
are kind and compassionate to the stranger
and the outcast, live simply, and care for the other.
We will no longer serve that which does not serve us
nor avoid the safety of silence.
We will know love and friendship
are the frontiers of what humans can achieve.
For better or worse, this will be our home;
this will be our family.
In this garden, sit still with me
as our souls sing a silent song of gratitude to life.

How do I envision ...

What you leave behind
is not what is engraved on stone monuments
but what is woven into the lives of others.
—Pericles

How do I envision

the last days of my life
and what do I want?
I don't want to be in a hospital;
I want to be at home
still sitting up loving the tree tops,
the ever-changing sky,
the heron or goose flying by.
I want to be part of nature—
not a name on a chart—
joined to and grounded by that which
has given me the greatest pleasure in life.
I want to be in my place of sanctity and healing—
that grove of purple and white lilacs
which is safe, private, powerful,
and fills me with grace.

Belonging

1

The more I love this natural world,
the readier I am to die
since I feel so much a part of it
on this side and, I believe,
will be on the other.

2

Nature's unique gift to humankind
is consciousness.
What have I, for one, done with that—
including the knowledge
of my impending death?

3

If you knew me,
look for me now among those
whom I affected for the better
and pardon the hurt I caused—
for I was a clumsy learner
searching for what matters most.

4

Young friend, as I watch you
walk the tightrope of your life,
my stomach churns.

Often, I despair ...

The more I know,
the crazier this world seems.
How do I then hang onto
my own equanimity?
I remain grateful for the sky,
the trees, the birds—forgetting
they, too, are dying out.
Do I stay sane in this insane world
by focusing on my own survival
while caring for a few others,
as some always have
in other desperate situations?

About death

Elsewhere you are a guest.

To us, you are the secret
we don't want to know—

the one to hide from,
try to defeat, bargain with.
You overwhelm, empty, overshadow.
Haunt and feel bleak.
In your company, we are alone.
Yet some look you in the eye,
remember and find meanings.

When you are accepted,
you inspire healing, gratitude,
transformation.
You bring peace,
cast rainbows and encourage
honesty.

The picture turns right-side up
and love is offered and received.
You arrive in your own particular
inopportune way,
sit beside us as time slows
to await the moment when breath stops.

You leave a vacuum
that is filled with stories, hurts,
regrets, tendernesses, abandonments,
silence.

You reap indiscriminately
yet give many a pass.
Are you simply blind?
Not on the side of evil?
Or do you lack agency
and are a neutral necessity of life?
How are your choices made?

When do you know
that you've come at the wrong time
or for the wrong person?
That a mistake is being made?
Will you then walk alongside,

not saying anything, be a companion
and decide this is only a visit?

Do you know if we die
the way we lived?
Is your work easier if we find
redemption, wisdom, peace, meaning
before we face you?
Or grace?

How I have touched others
will live on after me.
And so, with them.
We remain
even as you take us with you.
There is no nonbeing.
Only life is impermanent.

How I want to die

1

I want to die at home.
It is where I feel at ease—
comfortable, safe, and protected.
My plants are here, my Buddhas,
my books, my CDs, my photos.
And outside my window are my bird feeder,
the willow trees, and the sky.
All these hold good memories
and connect me to my life.
Home is also my community—
people who know me
and some who care about me.
But I don't want to linger.
If I become a burden
or my condition prevents me from staying,
then I would go to a hospice

and, finally, want an assisted death.
Under no circumstances do I want to end up in a hospital.
Instead, let me smell the earth, enjoy the sunshine,
and play me some Beethoven.

2

Am I unreasonable?
Asking for too much?
I don't think so.
In fact, this way of dying
is simpler, less expensive,
and involves less suffering and anguish
than a prolonged hospital death.
Shall I go along with what others
think is best for me?
Or remember that fear deforms the soul
and do what is right for me—is me?
If there has to be suffering,
then there should be a purpose to it.
But if that suffering has no meaning,
why not do what is right for me instead?
Show up as I am and die as my self.
I resolve not to forget this when fear wakes me up
at three in the morning.

Notes from above ground

1

Dying can take years
and I may only be at its beginning.
This morning I am in a daze
considering the complexity
of my illness and its implications.
Who will be there for me?
Will the future be worth living?
I don't want to be the one
who will not die.

New snow is falling and I welcome
the cardinals and grossbeaks to my feeder.
Fear can wait.

2

In the dining room
no one talks about how they feel
about the son who steals from them,
the doctor who with his retirement forsakes them,
the difficulty of bringing a fork to mouth,
or walking without falling.
Let alone the loneliness or the anxiety
about the headache that doesn't go away.

3

How to read the signs,
to understand what is happening?
To be reassured that it will be alright—
at least for now.
Those who know are so cautious
and have so little time.
Life will go on without me.
They'll say, "He crossed the threshold.
He's on the other side."
As though I simply moved
to a different, probably happier realm.

4

I wish for an easy death,
little suffering, a quick decline
with not too much work for those around me.
To enter a deep "sleep,"
then breathe more and more slowly,
and finally, be still.
"Is he gone?" someone will say.
"I think so," another will answer.

They'll call my doctor,
and later my friends will sing me out,
which is our custom,
as I leave in a pine box.

To my power of attorney for personal care

Is that dark secret mine alone
or do you, too, fear the approach
and coming near of death
out of the shadows where we have hidden it
to keep us safe and tried to elude its inevitability?
Why can't it wait until I'm ready
or, better still, we've defeated it?
Right now, I deserve some hope—
for more time, for a breakthrough,
a spontaneous remission.
At least my doctors don't talk about dying.
They are matter of fact, manage my symptoms,
behave as though all this happens every day
(which it does). But I feel alone, stifled,
silenced, anxious, sad. Is this all there is
to a life and its ending?
This emptiness, this pretending, these secrets?
What can I do to bring meaning
into the Now I have left?

How can I face death directly?
Recall the worth of my life
and take comfort in it?
Is there an object, a talisman,
I want near me in these last days?
And what do I still need to say and heal
before I die? I wish for a guide,
someone who knows the terrain
of this final stage of my life—
who will help me navigate its terrors
and be present to its surprises.
Someone who can help me know

when enough is enough
and decide it is time to go.
I don't want to suffer or lose my dignity.
Most certainly, I don't want to die alone,
neglected and overtreated in a hospital hallway.
As happens often.
Please respect me:
ensure that I stay at home.
Make me comfortable,
listen to me, be with me.
Moisten my lips, hold my hand,
stroke my face and play me Beethoven sonatas.
I would love to hear from those to whom I mattered
and for whom I cared.
And do not hesitate to remind me to let go
when my body is ready.
Need I say, I also value being together
with you in silence.

And I arrive at a place
where the real and the imagined
blur and blend,
dissolve into a trace.
Much as you search for me now,
you will not find me
for I am as ethereal
as a tale that was never told.

Author Overview

Gregory Sass emigrated with his family from war-torn Germany to Canada at age sixteen. *The Canadian Forum* published his first poems the following year.

In 1956 he met George Drew, former Premier of Ontario and then Leader of the Opposition in Parliament. When Mr. Drew asked Greg what he planned to do after high school graduation, Greg told him he couldn't afford to go to university. Mr. Drew suggested Greg become a Cana soldier through the Regular Officers' Training Plan. This required Canadian citizenship which Greg received by Act of Parliament thanks to Mr. Drew.

After getting two degrees, Greg worked as an editor, teacher, manager at TVOntario, social worker, and psychotherapist. Throughout, he wrote and published nine books — Canadian history, special education, and poetry.

Today, the leisure of retirement has given him the luxury to enjoy what he values: the silence within; sunrise and sunset; birdsong; reading; writing; quality conversation; being kind to whoever needs it and supporting causes he believes in.

Soul's Journey is the poetic story of his own inner life lived during significant turning points in our time. It is an authentic, compelling tale of resilience, survival, and overcoming that leads to a life rich in meaning and loving relationships. ----------------

9 781774 033258